Colorado

A Guide To The
State & National Parks

Barbara Sinotte

HUNTER
PUBLISHING

Hunter Publishing, Inc.
300 Raritan Center Parkway
Edison NJ 08818, USA
Tel (908) 225 1900
Fax (908) 417 0482

ISBN 1-55650-740-2

Maps by Kim André

Cover photo by JC Leacock

Springtime. La Plata Mountains, CO

Other titles in the Parks Series include:
ARIZONA & NEW MEXICO, CALIFORNIA, COLORADO,
NEW YORK & NEW JERSEY, OREGON & WASHINGTON

Contents

A WORD ABOUT HIKING...
    Checklist For A Day Hike
    Hiking Safety

COLORADO

Camping	2
Rafting	3
Fishing	3
Hunting	3
Passes & Permits	4
Important Addresses	4

STATE PARKS

Barbour Ponds State Park	7
Barr Lake State Park	9
Boyd Lake State Park	11
Castlewood Canyon State Park	15
Chatfield State Park	17
Cherry Creek State Park	21
Colorado River State Park	24
Corn Lakes	26
Connected Lakes	26
Island Acre	27
Mill Tailing Site	28
Colorado River Wildlife Area	28
Colorado State Forest & Park	29
Crawford State Park	32
Eldorado Canyon State Park	35
Golden Gate Canyon State Park	38
Harvey Gap State Park	42
Highline State Park	44
Jackson Lake State Park	46
Lathrop State Park	49
Walsenburg Golf Club	51
Mancos Lake State Park	51
Mueller State Park	53
Navajo State Park	56
North Sterling State Park	59
Paonia State Park	62

Spinney Mountain State Park   64
Stagecoach State Park   66
Steamboat & Pearl Lake State Park   69
Sweitzer Lake State Park   71
Sylvan Lake State Park   74
Trinidad State Park   76
Vega State Park   78

NATIONAL PARKS
Mesa Verde National Park   85
The Anasazi Family   85
History   85
Visiting the Park   87
Balcony House   89
Cliff Palace   90
Spruce Tree House   91
Park Point   92
Fire Lookout   92
The Mesa   93
Establishment of Mesa Verde National Park   94
Caphin Mesa Archaeological Museum   94
The National Register of Historic Places   96
Lodging   96
Camping   96
Rocky Mountain National Park   98
Visitor Centers   98
Back Country Camping/Bouvac Camping   99
Accommodations Services   99

A Word About Hiking...

Hiking is by far the most popular activity in state and national parks. Most hiking involves following clearly marked trails. Off-trail travel (commonly referred to as bushwhacking) is practiced by the more adventurous hikers – especially in the less populated areas of parks.

Trails in many state parks have been rated by combining distance and degree of difficulty. If you are not sure which trails are appropriate for you and your family, talk to a park ranger. If you do not exercise regularly, start on beginner trails and increase distances gradually. Trail maps are usually available either at the trail head or at the ranger station.

While trail markings vary widely, there are a few common markings with which you should be familiar. Paint blazes on trees or rocks are clearly the most popular form of trail markings. Plastic markers are often nailed to trees or metal signs are hung on wooden posts. Often trails are marked with piles of rocks.

Watch for trail markers and make a habit of it – for your own safety and the safety of those hiking with you. It will soon become just another "natural" thing to do.

If you want to attempt bushwhacking, be careful. Make your first attempts in open areas with limited undergrowth – such as a desert area where the terrain is a little easier to tackle. Bushwhacking through areas of dense vegetation is for the more experienced and should only be attempted with map, water, and compass in hand.

Bushwhacking or carefully following trails, setting a pace will make the experience enjoyable for you. You are not in a race and can better take in the surroundings if you are walking at a comfortable speed. Remember that attempting to go too fast can burn you out before you are half-way through your hike. Stumbling or tripping is a sign that you may need to slow your pace.

Remember to take frequent rests. Don't wait for fatigue to tell you it's time. Use this rule of thumb: a 10- to 15-minute stop every hour or so is a good idea to begin. After a while you will know what is best for you.

Don't speed over the rough areas of a trail. Watch out for tree roots and damp, old logs. Alternate footings should be sought. When you are uncertain of your footing, it is wise to crouch, lowering your center of gravity to reduce the likelihood of falling. Steep trails will cause hikers to lose their balance and take a tumble. Descending tends to be more hazardous and requires a little more attention than ascending. Use small trees or rocks to hold onto. When in doubt, sitting and easing your way down on your rear might be the way to go.

When hiking with a family, it is important to choose a trail that is comfortable for everyone. Younger children should be introduced to hiking with short walks. It is more fun and educational if they can be involved in planning the hike.

Checklist For A Day Hike

2 pair of hiking socks
Liner socks
Long pants
Long sleeved shirt
Shell parka or windbreaker
Hiking boots
Day pack
Water bottle
Waterproof poncho
Extra sweater
Snack foods
Toilet paper
Plastic litter bag
Map
Trail guidebook
Compass
First aid kit
Flashlight
Pocket knife

In warm weather add:
T-shirt
Shorts
Extra water

Bug repellant
Sunscreen or lotion
Sun hat

In cool or cold weather add:
Additional layers
Cap or hat
Thermal underwear
Matches
Watch

Hiking Safety

- ❑ Hike with a friend.
- ❑ Take plenty of drinking water.
- ❑ Let someone at the camp or at home know where you are going and when you plan to return.
- ❑ Don't take shortcuts on switchback trails.

Colorado

Colorado has the highest elevation of any state in the Union. Three-quarters of the nation's land above 10,000 ft. is located here. Colorado has 54 mountains 14,000 ft. or higher ("the Fourteeners"), and about 830 mountains between 11,000 and 14,000 ft. The state encompasses the highest portion of the Rocky Mountains. It is not suprising that many think of mountains when Colorado is mentioned. Colorado has impressive canyons, too – but most hikers look upward.

Colorado offers hikers and backpackers everything from quiet streamside trails to remote wilderness adventures. Many hunters and fishermen feel the region was made for them. Rafting has become so popular that trips are rationed on some streams. The 4-wheel-drive vehicle is utilized here for back country travel. Aspen and Steamboat Springs are only two of the several winter sports centers. By far the most popular outdoor activity is sightseeing, and there is much to see.

The state's lowest point is 3,350 ft., where the Arkansas River flows into Kansas. The high plains slope gradually upward for 200 miles from the eastern border to the base of the Rocky Mountain foothills. Two-fifths of the land area is occupied by these plains.

Then come the mountains, occupying another two-fifths of the state. From the plains, foothills rise to the towering peaks behind them (7,000-9,000 ft.). Beyond the Front Range are other ranges, generally oriented north to south but with many spurs and extensions in other directions. The Continental Divide follows a wandering course from north to south through the state, roughly dividing the mountainous region in half, with rivers on one side flowing to the Pacific, those on the other to the Gulf of Mexico. Among some ranges are "parks " – open areas of relatively flat land. In the south-central area, between the San Juan Mountains and the Sangre de Cristo Range, is the broad San Luis Valley, crossed by the Ridge Grande River.

West of the mountains are high mesas, some above 10,000 ft., which extend to the Utah border. Deep canyons cut into the mesas.

Colorado's climate is cool and invigorating. During summer the plains can be hot, but relief often comes with afternoon thunder-showers. The mountains are almost always cool, with chilly to cold nights. Humidity is low, and the thin air heats quickly; skiers often wear light clothing. Conditions, however, are not constant through-out the state. Wide climatic variations can be experienced within short distances – horizontal or vertical. The difference in annual mean temperatures on Pikes Peak and at Las Animas, 90 miles away, is about the same as between Iceland and southern Florida.

Snow does not halt mountain travel here as it does in the Sierra Nevadas, where many passes are closed for the winter. Of 36 mountain passes, only three are closed during winter, two on the Trail Ridge Road in Rocky Mountain National Park, and Inde-pendence Pass where SR 82 crosses the Continental Divide. Snow does close much of the high back country to hiking and horse riding.

Over two-thirds of the state of Colorado is defined as National Forest land with more than 400 public campgrounds. The best backpacking areas include Rocky Mountain National Park, Pikes Peak, west of Denver in the Mt. Evans area, and the Rabbit Ears Pass area near Steamboat Springs. For more information contact the US Forest Service or Bureau of Land Management.

Camping

Colorado is teeming with camping sites. Most public camp-grounds are equipped with water, tables, benches, fire grates, gar-bage containers, and toilet facilities (no showers). Private campgrounds offer electrical and plumbing hook-ups, showers, laundry facilities, and often a swimming pool and clubhouse. For more information contact the US Forest Service or Bureau of Land Management.

Rafting

*M*ore than 40 whitewater rafting companies are operating in Colorado and thousands of adventurers flock to the state each year in search of the ideal rafting adventure. There are hundreds of miles of river in Colorado that can be rafted. For more information contact: Colorado River Outfitters Association, PO Box 1032, CR, Buena Vista, CO 81211.

Fishing

*M*ost of the 11,300 miles of streams and 2,400 lakes in Colorado are open to the public for fishing. A fishing license is required and available at sporting good stores as well as the Department of Wildlife.

The annual resident fishing license is $11 and $35 for non-residents. One-day stamps and two-day licenses are also available. The fishing season in Colorado lasts the entire year.

Hunting

*B*ig game hunting for elk, deer, antelope, bears, mountain lions, and mountain goats is enjoyed throughout Colorado. Some of the big game seasons limit licenses available through application and drawing. Others have unlimited licenses that can be obtained through the Division of Wildlife offices in Colorado.

Deer and elk season runs from October through November. Big horn sheep and mountain goat season opens in late August and antelope in September. Special archery, muzzleloading, and high country deer seasons are usually held prior to the regular deer and elk rifle season.

Passes & Permits

*A*ll vehicles entering a park are required to display a current Colorado state park pass on the windshield. A daily pass is valid from the day purchased until noon the following day. An annual pass is valid at any Colorado state park for the remainder of the calendar year. For annual pass holders who own another car, a duplicate pass is available for an additional fee. Passes are available at the park entrances and self-service dispensers.

Colorado residents 62 years of age or older qualify for a special Aspen Leaf Annual Pass available at a discounted rate. The Aspen Leaf Annual Pass allows free admission to all state parks every day and free camping on weekdays. A camping fee is charged on weekends and holidays.

Colorado disabled veterans displaying Colorado Disabled Veteran (DV) license plates are admitted free to state parks without a pass.

In addition to a parks pass, campers are required to purchase and display a camping permit at their campsite. Camping permits are available at main park entrances and self-service dispensers.

Please observe all posted rules and regulations for each State Park.

Important Addresses

Colorado State Parks
1313 Sherman St. #618
Denver, CO 80203
(303) 866-3437

Bureau of Land Management
2850 Youngfield
Lakewood, CO 80215
(303) 239-3600

Colorado Outfitter's Association
PO Box 440021
Aurora, CO 80044
(303) 841-7760

US Forest Service
740 Simms St.
Lakewood, CO 80225
(303) 275-5350

National Park Service
12795 W. Alameda Parkway
Lakewood, CO 80225
(303) 969-2000

For 24-hour-a-day season information on hunting and fishing;
☎ (303) 291-7299.

State Parks

Barbour Ponds State Park

Location: In the shadow of Longs Peak only 30 miles from Denver off I-25.

Although small, with only 50 land acres and 80 water acres, the park offers full-size recreational enjoyment. The setting is scenic and convenient, with large cottonwood trees for shade and a great view of Long's Peak. The park's four quiet ponds offer some of the best freshwater fishing in northern Colorado. The ponds are also stocked with rainbow trout in the spring and fall, creating a great fishery for all ages.

Surprisingly, the park began as a group of gravel pits dredged for highway construction – a far cry from the area's inviting appearance today. The reclamation began in 1962, when the Colorado Game, Fish and Parks Department obtained the area by trade from the highway department. The developing recreation area was named after Roy N. Barbour, a long-time Longmont resident and organizer of the Longmont Izaak Walton League. Since 1972, the Colorado Division of Parks and Outdoor Recreation has administered Barbour Ponds.

Picnics: Permitted throughout the park except in numbered campsites. There are tables and grills available around all the ponds. Large cottonwood trees provide shade for some of the sites.

Camping: Barbour Ponds offers 60 campsites located in two waterside campgrounds. Near the north end of the park lies a group site that can accommodate 12 units. Camping is only allowed in designated numbered sites. Be sure to display your camping permit in the marker at your campsite.

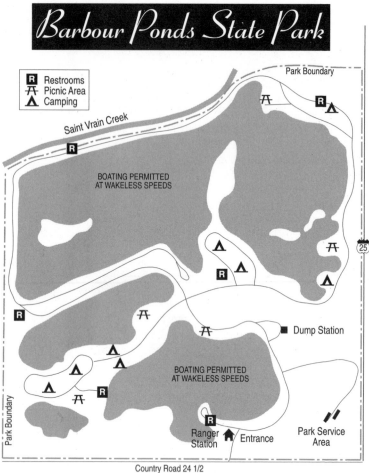

Boating: Only small vessels are permitted. Air-inflated devices are allowed if they contain more than one air compartment. Boaters at Barbour Ponds must observe the Colorado boating statutes and regulations, available in pamphlet form at the entrance station. Swimming is prohibited at Barbour Ponds.

Fishing/Hunting: The ponds contain bluegill, bass, channel catfish, and crappie. Rainbow trout are stocked in late March and late September. This program provides great fishing; the best times are just after stocking. No hunting due to the smallness of the park and close proximity to I-25.

Wildlife: Many opportunities exist for wildlife and nature study. The ponds are a habitat for large frogs and turtles, many kinds of waterfowl and wading birds, and interesting aquatic plants. Cattails, cottonwood trees, and willows are habitat for many songbirds. Bald eagles are sometimes seen during the winter.

There is a short nature trail near the park entrance that winds along the shore of one of the ponds. The entire land area of the park is fairly level and easily explored on foot. For guided walks or ranger-assisted nature hikes or talks, please contact the park.

Facilities for the Disabled: Because the area around the ponds is relatively flat, Barbour Ponds is accessible for the physically challenged, especially with some assistance. Concrete ramps lead to the two restrooms at the campground and to the restrooms at the park entrance.

For further information contact: Park Headquarters, Boyd Lake State Park, 3720 N. County Rd. 11C, Loveland, CO 80538. ☎ (970) 669-1739.

Barr Lake State Park

Location: From Denver, NE on 1-76. Just beyond Mile Marker 22, turn right. This turn and the next two are marked for the park, though not conspicuously.

A major prairie reservoir of over 1,900 acres forms the heart of this 2,600-acre park. The lake is lined with cottonwoods, marshes, and aquatic plants, and its southern half is designated as a wildlife refuge to shelter animals and a variety of birds unequaled elsewhere in Colorado. In the late 1880s, Barr Lake was an elite outing area for sportsmen from Denver. It was touted as the "finest fishing area in the west." Later, pollution almost ruined the lake. Fortunately, laws and controls that have been in effect since the 1960s helped to stop the flow of pollution into the lake. Water storage and irrigation continue to be the primary uses for the lake. This results in extreme seasonal fluctuation of the lake's water level. Since the early 1900s, Barr Lake has been known as a premier bird watching area. Approximately 330 species of birds have been seen at the lake, making it internationally famous. Recently, it has gained fame for hosting one of only a few successful nests of bald eagles on the front range.

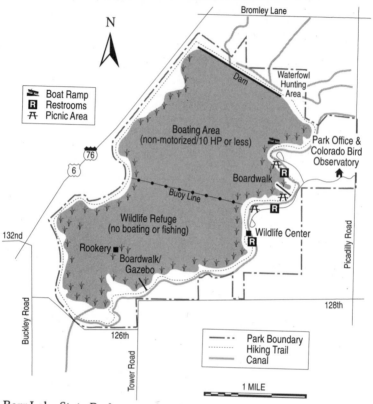

Barr Lake State Park opened to the public in 1977. It is administered by the Colorado Division of Parks and Outdoor Recreation.

Recreation at Barr Lake harmonizes with nature. It is a park to drive to, not to drive through. Visitors may boat, fish, hike, bicycle, horseback ride, participate in nature study, birdwatch and, in winter, cross-country ski.

Trails: A nine-mile trail follows the perimeter of the lake. Shorter walks may be made to the boardwalks that extend over the lake. The southern boardwalk, a three-mile round trip from the south parking lot, extends out to a gazebo that provides an excellent view of the rookery at the lake's south end.

The Niedrach Nature Trail, which begins near the south parking lot, is a short loop trail leading from the main trail through an open field, along the lake shore and across a boardwalk over the lake.

Hikers are encouraged to use binoculars and spotting scopes to get a closer view of wildlife.

Bicycles: Permitted on the main trails but not on the boardwalks. The trail is not paved and thorns are prevalent. Bicyclists are encouraged to use bikes with thorn-proof tires.

Horseback Riding: Visitors may ride their horses on park trails. Horses are not permitted on boardwalks.

Boating: Only sailboats, hand-propelled crafts, and boats with electric trolling motors or gasoline motors (10 horsepower or less) are permitted on Barr Lake. Boats are allowed only on the north half of the lake. The wildlife refuge is separated from the boating area by a line of buoys. A boat ramp is located adjacent to the north parking lot. Swimming, wading, and diving are prohibited.

Fishing: Channel catfish, small and large-mouth bass, rainbow trout, walleye, bluegill, wiper, and tiger musky are among the species that have been stocked at Barr Lake by the Colorado Division of Wildlife. Review the current Colorado Fishing Regulations for special restrictions.

Nature Study: Barr Lake State Park offers the nature enthusiast a remarkable opportunity to observe all types of wildlife, including fox, deer, and such dramatic birds as white pelicans, great blue herons, cormorants, egrets, ducks, grebes, owls, eagles, and hawks.

Park rangers offer interpretive programs and guided walks that enable visitors to learn about all aspects of the park, from its history to the plants and wildlife that make it a unique area. Programs such as early morning walks or night astronomy sessions are offered frequently. Information about upcoming programs is available at the park office or at ☎ (303) 659-6055.

The park serves as the headquarters for the Colorado Bird Observatory. Conservation of birds through research and education is CBO's goal. Their staff operates banding stations in the park, offers public programs, and is a valuable source of information. They can be reached at ☎ (303) 659-4348.

The Wildlife Center is near the south parking lot. It is administered by the Colorado Division of Wildlife. Visitors to the center can see displays about the park's wildlife and have questions answered by a staff naturalist. Programs and walks are offered through the center, and information about these may be obtained at ☎ (303) 659-1160. Center hours vary seasonally.

Winter Recreation: Cross-country skiing and snowshoeing are permitted on the park's trails. Due to unstable ice conditions, extreme caution is advised for ice activities. Visitors are required to remain on the trails in the wildlife refuge year-round.

Waterfowl Hunting: Waterfowl hunting is permitted only during the legal waterfowl seasons and only on certain days of the week. This activity is restricted to blinds located north of the dam. Registration is required. Two specially designed blinds are available for physically challenged hunters. Contact the park office for current hunting restrictions and information.

No other hunting or trapping is permitted in the park.

For further information contact: Park Superintendent, Barr Lake State Park, 13401 Picadilly Road, Brighton, CO 80601. ☎ (303) 659-6005.

Boyd Lake State Park

Location: One mile east of Loveland. Follow US 34 west of I-25, turning north on Madison Avenue. Watch for the signs leading to the park.

Boyd Lake State Park is a water-sports haven for northern Colorado. The park attracts visitors who enjoy boating, waterskiing, swimming, fishing, windsurfing, bicycling, walking, hunting, and wildlife viewing. The park features camping and picnicking. The lake lies at the westernmost edge of the plains at the foot of snow-capped Long's Peak and the mountains of the Continental Divide. Sunrises and sunsets are spectacular when clouds illuminate the eastern horizon and mountain peaks. Boyd Lake contains nearly 1,800 surface acres when full. The reservoir provides drinking water for the city of Greeley and irrigation to Colorado farms.

Boyd Lake
State Park

N

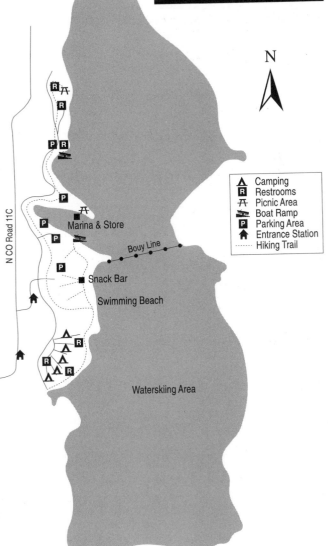

⛺	Camping
R	Restrooms
⛱	Picnic Area
🚤	Boat Ramp
P	Parking Area
⌂	Entrance Station
····	Hiking Trail

N CO Road 11C

Marina & Store

Bouy Line

Snack Bar

Swimming Beach

Waterskiing Area

Boating/Skiing: Boyd Lake has two paved launch ramps. A six-lane ramp is located north of the beach, while a two-lane ramp is located just north of the group picnic area. The entire lake is open to boating and sailing. Only the south end of the lake is open to waterskiing. The ski pattern is counter-clockwise. Boaters must observe the Colorado boating statutes and regulations.

Swimming: The Boyd Lake beach provides cool relief on Colorado's warm summer days. A pavilion at the beach includes showers, restrooms, a first-aid station, and a food concession. Float toys may be used in the buoyed-off swimming area.

Wildlife: Boyd Lake affords great opportunities to observe wildlife. Fox, beaver, coyote, and other small mammals are seen frequently by park visitors. The bird population includes great blue heron, egrets, great-horned and burrowing owls, hawks, eagles, white pelicans, as well as other species. The changing seasons bring a variety of wildlife to Boyd Lake.

Walking/Bicycling: Walking and biking can be enjoyed on the paved, grassy trails that run along beaches, under cool cottonwood trees, and to the water's edge. Trails join with the city of Loveland's regional trail system at the south and north ends of the park. During the winter, the trails can be used by cross-country skiers.

Fishing: Boyd Lake is a popular spot with anglers for bass, catfish, crappie, perch, rainbow trout, and walleye. During the winter, ice fishing is a favorite pastime. Underwater ridges and inlet areas can produce great fishing when the water is flowing. A Colorado fishing license is required. Division of Wildlife regulations apply.

Waterfowl Hunting: Waterfowl hunting is permitted at Boyd Lake during Colorado's legal waterfowl seasons, with a valid Colorado waterfowl hunting license. Hunting on the ice when ice conditions permit is allowed. Contact the park office for hunting restrictions and information.

Camping: Boyd Lake offers 148 paved, pull-through campsites. The sites are located on a grassy, tree-covered knoll near the lake. The easily accessible sites can accommodate tents, pick-up campers, trailers, and motor homes. Each site has a picnic table and grill. Playground equipment and horseshoe pits are scattered throughout the campground. There are three restrooms with showers.

Campers must have a camping permit and a parks pass. Please camp only in designated sites and display the campground permit in the marker at your campsite.

A holding tank dump station is located in the campground. It is illegal to dump wastewater, including dishwater, anywhere except the dump station.

Picnicking: The park features 95 individual picnic sites on the west side of the lake, 15 of which are sheltered. There are 30 sites located at the beach and another 15 along the west shore between the campground and beach. There are 50 more sites at the north end of the park.

For further information contact: Park Superintendent, Boyd Lake State Park, 3720 North County Road 11-C, Loveland, CO 80538. ☎ (970) 669-1739.

Castlewood Canyon State Park

Location: Take I-25 to Castle Rock, turn east on Highway 86. Go six miles to Franktown, turn south on Highway 83 (S. Parker Rd.) and go five miles south to the park entrance.

Castlewood Canyon State Park, an 873-acre day-use area, offers a variety of activities in an ecological setting. This scenic canyonland of the high plains has a spectacular panoramic view of the Front Range and Pikes Peak. The park preserves a portion of the Black Forest and its vegetative communities and wildlife habitats.

A trail leads to the ruins of the Castlewood Canyon Dam, built in 1890 for irrigation purposes. On August 3, 1933 the dam collapsed and was responsible for two deaths and $1 million in damages.

From sunrise to sunset, Castlewood Canyon State Park is open for sightseeing, picnicking, hiking, photography, nature study, and technical rock climbing.

Hiking/Trail Use: Please stay on designated trails. Mountain bike use is restricted to roads and designated bike trails. No horseback riding is allowed on the trails.

Rock climbing: The installation of bolts and fixed protection is prohibited. Please use designated trails for access.

Regulations: A complete copy of park regulations is available at the ranger station.

Facilities: East side – includes a visitor center, a spectacular canyon-view nature trail, flush toilets, picnic areas, and group picnic area. Most facilities on the east side of the park are accessible and barrier-free. West side – includes parking, one pit toilet, and 20 picnic tables.

For further information contact: Park Superintendent, Castlewood Canyon State Park, PO Box 504, Franktown, CO 80116. ☎ (303) 688-5242.

Chatfield State Park

Location: South of Denver on Wadsworth Blvd. past County Line Road, C-470. Turn west into the Deer Creek entrance.

The first settlers came to the Chatfield area in search of gold in 1858. Prospectors discovered gold in the vicinity of nearby Cherry Creek and the South Platte River. When these pioneers began building the settlement that is now Denver, Indians warned them that it was "bad medicine" to settle in the area.

In 1870, Issac W. Chatfield, a Union lieutenant in the Civil War, bought 720 acres of land at the confluence of the South Platte River and Plum Creek. Chatfield farmed the land until he moved in1879. The area and a nearby road still use his name.

The area continued to grow as an agricultural community and small activity centers and subdivisions were built. But the warning of "bad medicine" proved true as floods rumbled through Denver in 1933, 1935, and 1942.

On June 16, 1965, the rain-swollen South Platte River overflowed and swept away homes and businesses. The result was 13 deaths and over $300 million in damages. Following that flood, citizens banded together with state and federal officials to get Chatfield Dam built as a flood control measure.

In August, 1967, two years after the flood, the US Army Corps of Engineers began construction on the $85 million project. Work began on the 5,600 acre recreation area in 1973, and in 1974 the Colorado Division of Parks and Outdoor Recreation leased the area for 25 years. The dam was completed in 1976, resulting in a 1,450-acre lake.

Hiking: A series of trails winds through the Chatfield area and provides the park visitor with an abundance of opportunities. You can take a morning jog, walk through natural areas around the reservoir, pedal your bicycle through the park, or ride a horse into the sunset. Trail maps may be obtained at the park's main entrances.

Picnicking: Numerous picnic sites with tables and grills are located throughout the park. Both group and individual sites are available on a first-come, first-served basis, but some group sites may be reserved by calling the park office.

Activities: A special area for hot air balloonists is Montgolfier Launch Site, located near the Deer Creek entrance. A balloon permit is required in addition to the parks pass for persons using the launch site.

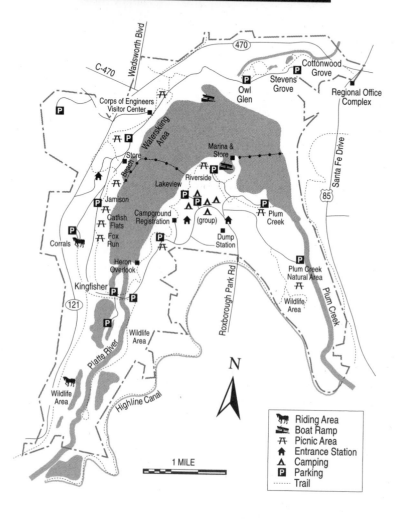

For model airplane pilots, Chatfield provides paved runways, frequency posts, and field regulations for radio-controlled aircraft in an area south of the campgrounds.

Water Sports: Boating, waterskiing, sailing, and swimming are among the most popular activities to cool a hot summer day. Areas are set aside for different activities to ensure maximum safety for everyone. There are designated waterski beaches and a swimming beach. Boaters must observe markers and zoning on the lake. Copies of the Colorado Boating Statutes and Regulations are available at park entrances and boat ramps.

Wildlife: Chatfield's thousands of acres of prairie grasses, water, and ground cover support a multitude of wildlife species. Over 180 species of birds have been sighted at Chatfield – most notably great blue herons. A 27-acre heron rookery is the bre cling area for over 50 pairs of the large birds. They can be viewed from the observation area, but for the protection of the endangered birds no one is permitted to enter the rookery during the nesting season. Beaver and muskrats often play in the water below, and whitetail and mule deer, coyotes, rabbits, and foxes also live or feed in the area.

Natural areas are located on the south side of the park along Plum Creek and the South Platte River. Check the park office for scheduling of interpretive walks and evening programs.

Facilities for the Disabled: Chatfield State Park is fully accessible to persons with disabilities. Twenty-five miles of paved trails are wide enough and level enough to accommodate wheelchairs. A fishing peir for the handicapped is located near the marina on the east side of the lake, and an access trail is located at the South Platte River.

Horseback Riding: Horsetrailer parking, corrals, unloading ramps, and the trail head are on the park's west side, most easily reached from the Deer Creek entrance. Horses may be leased at the Chatfield Livery, west of the beach, and trail maps are available at the park's main entrances.

Visitors may leave their horses in the corrals overnight if they are camping in the campground two miles from the corrals. Visitors must furnish their horse's feed, as grazing is not allowed. Water faucets are at the corrals. Riders must stay on designated trails; horses are prohibited at picnic sites, campsites, and the swimming beach.

Camping: Water faucets are conveniently located throughout the campground, and each of the 153 individual sites has a fire ring and grill. A camping permit is required in addition to the parks pass for persons using the campgrounds. Campers may stay a maximum of 14 days in any 45-day period, and immediate occupancy of sites is required. Quiet tours are observed from 10 PM to 6 AM, and generators may not be operated during these hours. A sewage dump station is located near the campground. Please use this facility. It is illegal to dump waste or sewage, including dishwater, anywhere else.

Individual sites can be reserved, and group sites are by reservation only. Further information can be obtained by calling the park office.

Fishing: In addition to a healthy population of trout and bass, Chatfield has channel catfish, yellow perch, crappie, bluegill, sunfish, and carp. The lake is periodically stocked with rainbow trout and other fish by the Division of Wildlife.

Springtime at Chatfield signals the start of open-water fishing; trout fishing is superb. Throughout the summer, bass, perch, crappie, catfish, and an occasional trout are caught, with the best action early and late in the day.

As fall brings cooler temperatures, the fish begin to feed more often, and the trout return from deep water into the shallows. Good trout fishing continues until the lake freezes.

For further information contact: Park Superintendent, Chatfield State Park, 41500 N. Roxborough Park Rd., Littleton, CO 80125. ☎ (303) 791-7275.

Cherry Creek State Park

Location: Take I-25 south out of Denver until it intersects I-225 at Parker Rd. Follow the clearly marked signs.

The recreational opportunities are unlimited at this 3,915-acre park. There's excitement on the 880-acre reservoir with water-skiers, windsurfers, and boaters. Yet solitude can be found fishing in a cove or walking the nature trails. For the most relaxing visit try the park on weekdays or evenings when Cherry Creek's atmosphere is quite different than on weekends.

The views are pretty spectacular, too. During the summer, colorful masts from sailboats and windsurfers dot the lake against a backdrop of the Rockies. It's a unique place. A fast getaway for city dwellers, it provides a place to learn about nature, a place to have a family picnic, and even a special area to train your dog.

Then there's the unexpected – a herd of over 100 deer, coyotes, pheasants, cottontails, and jackrabbits.

Cherry Creek Reservoir was built in 1950 by the Army Corps of Engineers to prevent flooding. The early settlers that travelled on the Smoky Hill Trail that cuts through Cherry Creek would have had a hard time imagining that this rolling prairie studded with yucca would become such an important natural resource to the people of Colorado.

Fishing: Head out to Cherry Creek to catch trout, walleye, bass, crappie, pike, carp, and catfish. The Tower Loop area near the dam is a popular spot, as is as the quiet south end of the reservoir. State record walleye have been caught at the reservoir.

Lake zoning maps and copies of current Colorado boating regulations are available at park entrances.

Bicycle Trails: Cherry Creeks extensive trail systems and bike lanes are a popular workout spot year-round. The trail system accesses other surrounding trail systems.

The Marina: The west side marina can make a sailor, windsurfer, or waterskier out of the eager-to-learn with lessons and rentals.

Boaters will find additional conveniences there – slip rental and fuel. Quench your thirst or get a snack at the food concession.

Horseback Riding: Horse rental and boarding are available at the stables near the east gate entrance. Miles of trails offer equestrians a real treat. Horse owners find it a good place to condition their horses. Call the stable at ☎ (303) 690-8235.

Decal: Also required for entry is a Cherry Creek Basin Water Quality Authority decal. The decal, which is $3 per year per vehicle, is required on all vehicles. The funds from the surcharge will be utilized to improve the water quality at Cherry Creek Reservoir.

Picnicking: Picnicking in the shade of tall cottonwoods at the Dixon's Grove area of Cherry Creek offers visitors a cool place for a family outing. Additional shade shelters, tables and grills are located throughout the park at waters' edge. ☎ (303) 690-1166 to reserve one of several group picnic sites.

Winter Recreation: Cherry Creek State Park can provide a special experience for the winter outdoors fan – ice fishing, ice skating and, as snow permits, cross-country skiing. Be sure and check ice conditions at the entrance stations.

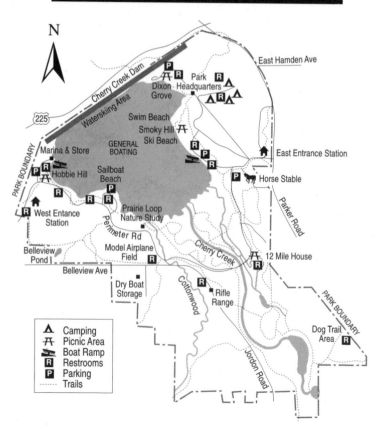

Camping: Cherry Creek offers metro-Denver area residents the convenience of close-in camping at its 102 sites located on the east side of the reservoir. Showers and laundry facilities are available, as well as limited electrical hook-ups. Campsites can be reserved in advance by ☎ (303) 470-1144 in the Denver Metro or ☎ (800) 678-CAMP outside Denver. Quiet hours are observed within the campground from 10 PM to 6 AM. A holding tank dump station is located across from the campground entrance. Please use this facility – it is illegal to dump waste and sewage, including dishwater.

Shooting Range: Fixed targets for rifles and pistols and a trap area for shotguns can be found in the southwestern corner of the park (☎ 303-693-1765). Firearms are prohibited elsewhere. Hunting is not allowed.

Model Airplane Field: Model airplane enthusiasts will find asphalt runways, frequency posts, and field regulations for radio controlled aircraft at this area located in the southwestern end of the park.

Swimming Beach: A gathering spot for young people to soak up that Colorado sun, Cherry Creek has a sandy beach and roped-off swimming area. Where else can you sit on a beach mid-summer and view snow-capped peaks? Food concessions, bathhouse, and first-aid station are located at the beach area.

Facilities for the Disabled: Special facilities to accommodate handicapped persons are located at the fishing access areas, the Dixon Grove picnic area, the campground, the group picnic sites, and the beach. Parking for handicapped visitors is signed throughout the park.

For further information contact: Park Superintendent, Cherry Creek State Park, 4201 S. Parker Road, Aurora, CO 80014. ☎ (303) 690-1166.

Colorado River State Park

Location: Colorado River State Park follows the Colorado River for miles through Grand Junction and the Grand Valley at Colorado's western border.

The park is a result of efforts by the Grand Junction/Mesa County Riverfront Commission to restore the Colorado River corridor in Mesa County and make it a useable recreation resource by improving public access.

Colorado River State Park will link together all of the various trails in this area along the river corridor from Island Acres in the east to the Loma boat launch in the west. Along this trail system there are a number of small picnic sites and fishing areas managed by Colorado State Parks. This makes up Colorado River State Park.

The Island Acres section at the eastern end of the park has been managed by State Parks since 1968. The cool lakes and turf grass at Island Acres provide a comfortable and lovely setting for swimming, fishing, picnicking, and camping.

Corn Lake was acquired by State Parks in 1991. The area is popular for fishing, hiking, picnicking, and as a launch site for boaters and rafters into the Colorado River. A trail, part of Colorado River State Park, extends from Corn Lake two miles west to the Colorado River Wildlife Area. This wildlife area is owned jointly by the US Bureau of Reclamation and Colorado State Parks. It features hiking, fishing, wildlife observation and is an outdoor classroom for local school children.

Connected Lakes was opened to the public in the fall of 1993 as a section of the Colorado River State Park. The area offers fishing, picnicking, bird watching, and hiking on the many different trails.

Colorado River State Park offers outdoor enthusiasts an access to the Colorado River corridor. Whether you visit the park to rest or play, its diverse wildlife and recreational opportunities will entertain you.

Trails: Each of the park sections has trails to hike and bike. The Island Acres section has a ¾-mile, self-guided, hard-packed trail following the course of the Colorado River and giving hikers a view of the park while taking a pleasant stroll through the area's geological history. Corn Lake has a mile-long, hard-packed trail around the lake and along the Colorado River; this trail ties in with the wildlife area. Connected Lakes has about four miles of trails, some paved and some hard-packed. A connecting trail runs between the lakes along the Redlands Canal and the Colorado River.

Picnicking: Picnicking is a popular activity at every section of the park. Several cool, green picnic sites are available along the river and at the lake shores. There are shaded picnic sites at all of the park sections.

Water Sports: Hand-propelled crafts and boats with electric trolling motors are allowed at Connected Lakes and Island Acres. All boating is prohibited at Corn Lake. Swimming is available at Island Acres Lake No. 2 and will be available at Connected Lakes once the swimming beach is constructed. Duke Lake, Connected Lakes and Island Acres Lakes No. 1, 3 and 4 are open to fishing for non-motorized boating and boats with electric trolling motors only. Boats with gasoline motors are not permitted on any lake in the park.

Winter Recreation: During the winter the park is open for ice skating and ice fishing when ice conditions are safe. Cross-country skiing and winter camping are offered for the hardier visitor.

Fishing: Good rainbow trout fishing is available throughout the park March through May, September, and October, especially at Island Acres and Corn Lake. The Colorado Division of Wildlife stocks Island Acres Lakes No. 1, 3 and 4 and Corn Lake. (Fishing is not permitted in Island Acres Lake No. 2.) Catfish, bluegill, bass, and crappie may be caught year-round.

Duke Lake and Connected Lake are two of the few lakes in western Colorado stocked strictly with warm water fish – bass, bluegill, catfish, and an occasional crappie.

Wildlife: The best time for viewing wildlife is in the early morning and early evening. Waterfowl, shorebirds, birds of prey including osprey, bald and golden eagles, many different songbirds and other game birds such as dove and quail may be found at any section of the park. The careful observer may see mule deer, skunk, cottontail rabbits, and beaver, all of which are common to the park and the surrounding area. Hunting is NOT permitted in any of the park areas.

Camping: Island Acres is the only section offering camping. There is a 34-site campground that can accommodate either tents ormotorized campers. Campers must display a valid camping permit in the campsite markers provided. Camping is permitted in designated sites only.

Corn Lakes

The Corn Lake section of Colorado River State Park is a day-use area opening at 7 AM and closing at dark. Corn Lake, at 32 Road and the Colorado River, serves as headquarters for Colorado River State Park and the Colorado State Parks West Region office.

Corn Lake provides a launching site for boaters and rafters to the Colorado River. Trails provide access to the Colorado River and Corn Lake for fishing and are used by hikers and bicyclists. The park also offers picnic sites and restrooms accessible to the physically challenged. There is no charge for bicycle or pedestrian access to the park.

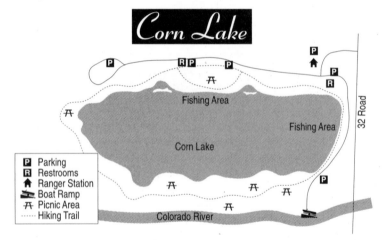

Connected Lakes

The Connected Lakes section of the Colorado River State Park is a day-use area, opening at 7 AM and closing at dark. The area can be accessed by traveling north and west on Dike Road off State Highway 340. Connected Lakes provides a network of trails traversing a series of gravel pits, giving visitors a wide variety of recreational opportunities including fishing, picnicking, hiking, and bird watching. There is no charge for bicycle or pedestrian access to the park.

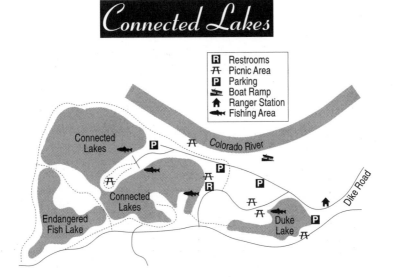

Island Acres

As the Colorado River and other erosional forces shaped the canyon, a large island was left in the middle of the river. The history of the canyon and its island reflects the history and constantly changing face of the West. A man-made dike, built in the 1950s, eliminated the true island characteristics of the area, but not its usefulness as a public recreation site. The park is now enjoyed by more than 85,000 visitors a year.

The Island Acres section is the only area of Colorado River State Park offering camping. The park is open year-round for camping and day-use activities with the day-use area closing at 10 PM. Island Acres is located at Exit 47 on Interstate 70 in the scenic Debeque Canyon. The park is a convenient and attractive place to fish, swim, camp, picnic, and hike along the Colorado River or near any of the lakes in the park.

Mill Tailing's Site

The mill tailings site was used in the late 1980s and early 1990s by the US Department of Energy to store uranium mill tailings until they were moved out of the area to permanent storage facilities. Colorado State Parks took over the site in 1994 once the mill tailings were removed. The area will be opened up to the public in the year 2000. The area will be another section of the park providing individual and group picnic areas, trails, playgrounds, and fishing access to the Colorado River.

Colorado River Wildlife Area

The area has one lake that allows restricted boating. Any non-motorized boating or boats with electric trolling motors are allowed west of the Island. Fishing is allowed on the lake and on the Colorado River.

The wildlife area is connected with Corn Lake by the main Colorado River trail. There are other trails taking visitors through the entire area. The trails are open to hiking, biking, and rollerblading. Motorized vehicles and horses are prohibited on the trails.

The area is planted with different types of food crops and habitat plantings for wildlife species. Waterfowl and upland game birds use the different habitats for feeding and nesting. Due to the nesting that occurs, sections of the trail are be closed to public use during certain times of the year.

For further information contact: Colorado River State Park, c/o Colorado State Parks, 313 Sherman Street #618, Denver, CO 80203. ☎ (303) 866-3437.

Colorado State Forest

Location: Two hours from Fort Collins. 75 miles west on Colorado Highway 14, past the famous Elephant Rock and over the Cameron Pass to the town of Gould.

Within the boundaries of the Colorado State Forest lie 70,000 acres of the great outdoors as it was meant to be. Mountain beauty greets the visitor and provides a setting unequaled for recreational possibilities – backpacking, hiking, horseback riding, lake and stream fishing, camping, four-wheeling, and relaxing.

The State Forest is high country, ranging in elevation from 8,500 to 12,500 feet. Visitors may find they need time to acclimate. Sunburn is possible in the high, thin, cool air and, until mid-summer, mosquito repellent is a necessity.

The park stretches along the west side of the Medicine Bow Mountains and into the north end of the Never Summer Range. From Ft. Collins, visitors can take Highway 14 over Cameron Pass – a 75-mile drive. From Denver, the route leads over Berthoud and Willow Creek passes to Walden – a 150-mile trip.

The State Forest's recreational uses are administered by the Colorado Division of Parks and Outdoor Recreation, which has leased the area for public recreation from the Colorado Board of Land Commissioners since 1972.

Camping: Ranger Lakes, The Crags, North Michigan Reservoir, and the Bochman campgrounds have 104 campsites which can accommodate tents, trailers, or pickup campers. Back country camping is allowed at various locations throughout the area and at Ruby Jewel, Kelly, Clear, and American lakes. Minimum-impact camping techniques are recommended at these alpine lake areas. No camping is allowed at Lake Agnes.

Campground users must have both a camping permit and a vehicle pass and must camp only in designated campsites. Display the camping permit in the site marker. Before camping in the back country, campers should check with a ranger or at the park office for information.

Cabins: The Colorado State Forest, a Colorado State Park, is the ultimate in rugged Colorado Wilderness. It offers visitors 70,000 acres of unaltered mountain country with vast stretches of forest, jagged peaks, and pristine alpine lakes. Camp, hike, fish, and hunt in an unspoiled, natural landscape away from crowds.

To make your visit even better, the Colorado State Forest boasts seven mountain cabins available for rent year-round. The cabins are rustic and can be part of a wonderful, back country vacation. The cabins are charming but basic, equipped with a wood-burning stove, wooden table, benches, and bunk beds with mattresses.

Colorado State Forest

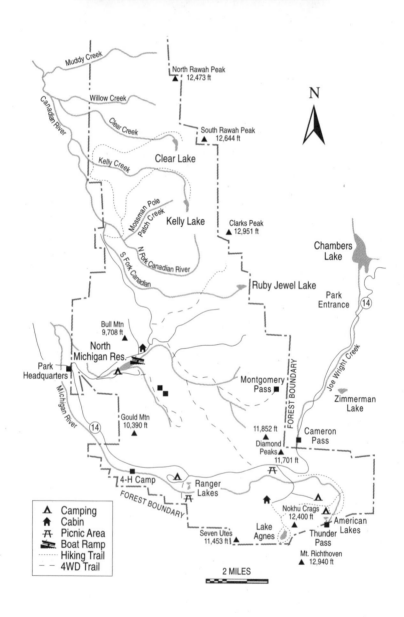

N

Muddy Creek

Willow Creek

Canadian River

Clear Creek

Kelly Creek

Clear Lake

North Rawah Peak
12,473 ft

South Rawah Peak
12,644 ft

Mossman Pole
Patch Creek

Kelly Lake

Clarks Peak
12,951 ft

N Fork Canadian River

S Fork Canadian

Ruby Jewel Lake

Chambers Lake

Park Entrance (14)

Bull Mtn
9,708 ft

North Michigan Res.

Park Headquarters

Michigan River

Gould Mtn
10,390 ft

(14)

Montgomery Pass

FOREST BOUNDARY

Joe Wright Creek

Zimmerman Lake

11,852 ft

Diamond Peaks
11,701 ft

Cameron Pass

4-H Camp

Ranger Lakes

FOREST BOUNDARY

Seven Utes
11,453 ft

Lake Agnes

Nokhu Crags
12,400 ft

Thunder Pass

American Lakes

Mt. Richthoven
12,940 ft

Legend

△ Camping
⌂ Cabin
🛤 Picnic Area
🚤 Boat Ramp
····· Hiking Trail
- - 4WD Trail

2 MILES

Outside, there are grills and picnic tables. There is no electricity, propane, running water, blankets, or bedding.

Six cabins are on the shore of North Michigan Reservoir the south end of the Forest. These cabins are accessible by vehicle all year. Winter visitors should expect difficult road conditions, particularly the last two miles. Winter conditions at the Forest can be extreme. Sub-zero weather and four to six feet of snow is not uncommon.

The Agnes Cabin is south of Colorado 14 on the west side of Cameron Pass. The access road is marked clearly along the highway The cabin is accessible over a rough road in summer, but in winter visitors must ski in. This two-mile trip is steep, finishing at 10,800 feet, and is considered difficult. ☎ (800) 678-2267 or (303) 470-1144 (Denver metro area) to reserve a cabin.

Boating: Boating is permitted only on North Michigan Reservoir. Power boats can be operated only at wakeless speeds. All other waters in the park are closed to boating.

Fishing: Brook, brown, native, rainbow, and golden trout are catchable. In North Michigan Reservoir and alpine lakes only artificial fly and lure fishing are permitted.

Vegetation: Lodgepole pine, spruce, fir, and aspen make up most of the forest. There are grassy meadows, sagebrush hillsides, and willowy stream courses. Tundra and alpine meadows are found above 11,000 feet. At all elevations throughout the park there is a vast array of colorful wildflowers in early summer, including the Colorado columbine.

Trailbikes/Four-Wheeling: Testing and spectacular runs are possible on the many miles of marked trails at the State Forest.

Motorized bikes must remain on designated trails. ATV's are not allowed to operate in the campgrounds or main park roads.

Hiking: Trails lead to Ruby Jewel, Kelly, Clear, Agnes, and American lakes. Camping and fires are not permitted at Lake Agnes. Please register at the trail registration boxes. A National Park Service back country permit is necessary if a backpacking trip is planned into Rocky Mountain National Park.

Horseback Riding: Visitors with horses frequently ride the back country. Groups may use the park for packtrips and horse camping. Horses are not allowed on the Agnes Trail or in the designated campgrounds. Contact the park office for information about pack-trips, horse rental, and horse camping.

Winter Recreation: Winter activities include cross-country skiing, snowshoeing and snowmobiling on a separate, extensive trail system. The snowmobiling trails are packed or groomed.

For further information contact: Park Superintendent, Colorado State Forest, Star Route, Box 91, Walden, CO 80480. ☎ (303) 723-8366.

Crawford State Park

Location: From Delta, take Colorado 93 to Hotchkiss. Continue on 92 and drive approximately 10 miles to Crawford. About one mile south follow signs to park.

Crawford State Park offers its visitors camping, fishing, watersports, hunting, and numerous other leisure activities in scenic mountainous terrain. The area around the park is almost exclusively cattle country. As the center of the cattle industry in the North Fork area, the nearby town of Crawford sees hundreds of cows herded down main street on their way either to market or a mountain pasture. Ranches and farms still surround the park drawing water from the same reservoir that affords visitors many recreational opportunities all year-round. The park's 6,600-ft. elevation guarantees visitors a mild climate at any season.

Within the boundaries of Crawford State Park are 337 land acres and the 400-acre reservoir, which was built in 1963 by the US Bureau of Reclamation. The Colorado Division of Parks and Outdoor Recreation has administered the area since 1965.

Camping: Crawford State Park offers 53 modern campsites. These can accommodate tents, trailers and campers. Tables, grills, and use pads are available at each campsite. Water hydrants are found in both main campgrounds.

Campers must have a camping permit and a parks pass, both available at the park entrances. Please camp only in designated sites and display the camping permit in the markers at your campsite. The campgrounds are patrolled for your safety. Quiet after 10

PM. For camping reservations, ☎ (303) 470-1144 in Denver and ☎ (800) 678-CAMP outside Denver.

Picnicking: Several picnic sites are located throughout the park, each with a grill or ring for fires.

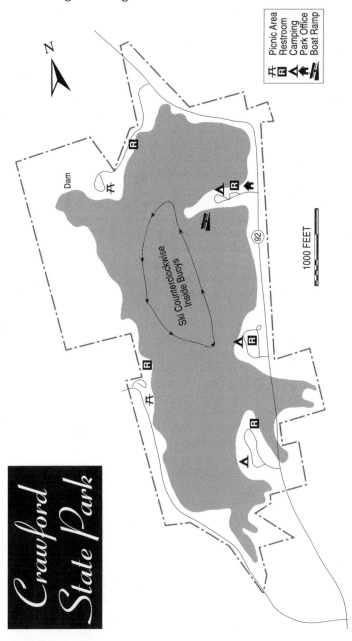

Boating/Water Recreation: Boaters at Crawford State Park are subject to Colorado boating statutes and regulations, which are available in pamphlet form at the entrance or on the boat ramp safety display.

Waterskiing season at Crawford usually begins in mid-May and ends in mid-August. Scuba diving is permitted in any safe area. A diver's flag is required.

Swimming is permitted in the swim area only.

Fishing: Crawford State Park is well known as a quality perch fishery. Largemouth bass and rainbow trout are stocked in the reservoir. Several record size catfish have also been caught here.

Fishing is permitted anywhere on the reservoir. Use or possession of minnows or fish for bait is prohibited.

Wildlife: Beavers, chipmunks, rabbits, and even mule deer live in or around the park and may frequently be seen at shoreline late in the evening.

A variety of waterfowl, from western grebes to graceful Canada geese, may be seen at Crawford State Park, either stopping off during migrations or nesting.

Winter Recreation: Cold weather enthusiasts come to Crawford State Park for ice fishing, ice skating, and snowmobiling.

For further information contact: Park Superintendent, Crawford State Park, Box 147, Crawford, Colorado 81415. ☎ (970) 921-5721.

Eldorado Canyon State Park

*Location: Just southwest of Boulder, follow Colorado 93 south to
Colorado 170. Turn west and continue through the town of
Eldorado Springs to reach the park.*

*H*idden in the foothills southwest of Boulder is a jewel of the State Park system, Eldorado Canyon. Bordered by the expansive Great Plains and the Rocky Mountains, Eldorado Canyon is a remarkable sight. Massive rock formations rise abruptly some 1,500 feet above the canyon floor. Snow-fed waters rage through the canyon's mid-section. Multi-colored lichens adorn the rock crags and Eldorado's sunlit, lichen-colored walls remind one of actual gold.

Ponderosa pines and Rocky Mountain juniper dot the drier south-facing slopes, while the north slopes are dominated by Douglas fir. The creek bottom is rich with water-loving plants like cottonwood, willow, and boxelder. Golden eagles soar high above while Abert's and golden mantled ground squirrels cavort under a forest canopy. Mule deer watch with a wary eye, while rainbow trout swim in the icy, emerald-colored waters.

The Inner Canyon has attracted visitors for centuries. Native Americans are known to have used the canyon for shelter; the sun-warmed walls provided a respite from winter winds. European man later settled the area and thrived on agriculture and lumbering. Then, in 1902, the Fowler family built a resort at the mouth of the canyon. People flocked to the naturally warm pools and to watch a highwire act some 350 feet above the canyon floor.

This natural landmark, evidence of the earth's restless history, was preserved as a State Park in 1978.

A natural setting such as a park can be a home for wild animals. We are only visitors to this home and should view them from a distance. The habitats of black bears and mountain lions are rarely seen by humans. Chance encounters with rattlesnakes and ticks can be reduced by staying on trails. Check for information at the trailheads on what to do if you encounter a wild animal.

The erosive topography at Eldorado Canyon is a prime scenic attraction but can also be a source of danger. Rock fall is common along trails, climbing routes, and vehicle access roads. Minimize these dangers by staying on maintained trails and by parking in the lots provided.

Trails: Trails in the park are open to a variety of non-motorized uses. Expect to see mountain bikes, horses, and hikers at any time. Check the trailheads for segregated-use information. Please respect other trail users as they may not be aware of your presence. Visitors unaccustomed to high elevations should allow more time to reach their destinations due to the effects of altitude. Trails are available for many park visitors. Physically challenged visitors may enjoy the Fowler Trail, which offers dramatic views of the inner canyon.

Eldorado Canyon
Inner Canyon

PARK BOUNDARY

PARK BOUNDARY

Eldorado Springs

Entrance Station

THE ROTWAND

Streamside Trail

The Bastille
6,100 ft ▲

THE WIND TOWER

HAWK EAGLE

Fowler Trail

Overlook ■

REDGARDEN WALL

Eagle Rock ■

THE WEST RIDGE

RINCON WALL

Shirttail Peak
7,5000 ft ▲

QUARTZITE RIDGE

Supremacy Rock ■

⛺ (group)

Eldorado Canyon Trail

Visitors Center ■ ⛺

600 FEET

Hiking: Area trails are gentle to moderate in difficulty and allow for commanding views. Unimproved access to technical rock climbing routes is not recommended for general hiking.

Rock Climbing: Climbers gather from around the world to challenge themselves on the rock walls of Eldorado Canyon. Tens of thousands of climbers scale the walls each year, but only a handful of serious accidents occur. Most of these incidents involve people with little or no experience who believe scrambling unroped up the rocks looks like fun. Rarely do experienced climbers get seriously hurt. For those wishing to try the sport or improve their skills, park concessionaires operate climbing schools and guide services. And information is available at the park visitor center.

It is important to be familiar with technical rock climbing regulations before beginning a climb. While technical climbs do not require registration, it is your responsibility to make sure someone reports your absence if you are overdue. Bolts, pitons, and other fixed gear are not maintained by the park. Climbers use these anchors at their own risk. Seasonal closings are implemented to protect raptors or "birds of prey" in the park. Closures and climbing regulations are posted at the trailheads. These regulations have been established to protect natural resources while allowing for a diversity of quality climbing experiences.

Mountain Bikes: Bikes are restricted to established roadways and Walker Ranch Loop in Crescent Meadows.

Picnicking: The snow-fed waters of South Boulder Creek wind through the canyon and under a cool forest canopy at the picnic area. Dotted along the stream are picnic sites complete with tables and picnic grills. Restrooms and drinking water are located nearby. Although designed for individual family use, the area is popular with groups. Call the park in advance if you plan to use the area with a large group.

Camping: Camping is not available in the park. Contact the Boulder Chamber of Commerce for area locations.

Hunting: Hunting is allowed in the posted areas of Crescent Meadows only. Manner of take and season is also restricted. Check with a ranger for further information.

Roads: Vehicle parking is available at both ends of the road that runs through the canyon. This narrow, multiple-use road has a 10%

grade. Primarily a one-lane road, it has few pullouts. Hikers, bikes, and motor-vehicles often use the road simultaneously. Please be patient and allow others adequate clearance. Remember that uphill traffic has the right-of-way.

Large vehicles such as buses, recreational vehicles, and horse trailers are asked to park in the streamside parking lot located near the east entrance. Due to congestion and rock fall potential, motor-vehicle parking is not permitted between the lower main parking lot and the West Ridge rock formation.

Motor-vehicle access is restricted during peak summer periods, primarily weekends and holidays.

For further information contact: Park Superintendent, Eldorado Canyon State Park, PO Box B, Eldorado Springs, CO 80025. ☎ (303) 494-3943.

Golden Gate Canyon State Park

Location: From Golden, north 2 miles on SR 93, then left 14 miles on Golden Gate Canyon Rd.

With more than 14,000 acres of beauty ranging in elevation from 7,600 to 10,400 ft., Golden Gate offers a variety of outdoor recreation opportunities within an hour's drive of the Denver area.

Many miles of trails, once used by Indians, trappers, gold miners, lumberjacks and homesteaders, invite you to see the park as it was more than 100 years ago. Along the trails you can see the diversity of plants and animals that live in the park as well as spectacular mountain scenery. From Panorama Point on the north end of the park, you can see more than 100 miles of snow-capped peaks along the Continental Divide, including Long's Peak, Mount Evans and the Indian Peaks.

Three hundred years ago, Indians traveled through Golden Gate Canyon in search of deer, elk, and bearberries. The Cheyenne and Arapaho tribes lived in the area that is now Golden, while the nomadic Utes lived throughout the mountain area.

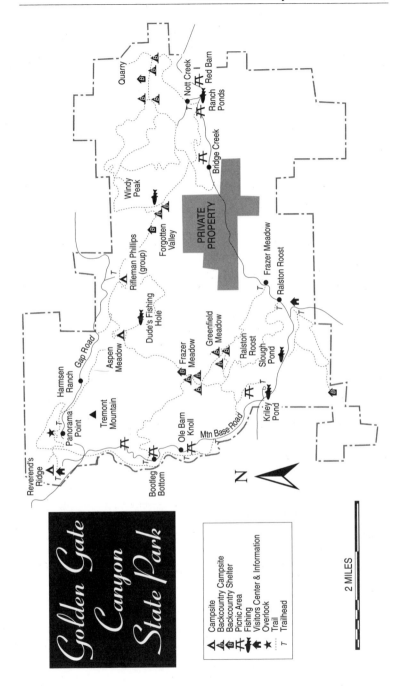

Golden Gate Canyon State Park

Campsite
Backcountry Campsite
Backcountry Shelter
Picnic Area
Fishing
Visitors Center & Information
Overlook
Trail
Trailhead

2 MILES

The next visitors to the area were trappers who came to hunt beaver in the early 1800s. However, the demand for beaver pelts was short-lived. By 1840 the trappers moved on and settlers moved into the area to farm and search for gold.

While there was no gold found in the area that is now the park, six miles to the south was a gold bonanza. Two gold camps, Black Hawk and Central City, grew quickly. To reach them, settlers built Golden Gate Road, which passes through the current park. By 1861, a road was built through Clear Creek Canyon and the Golden Gate Road deteriorated. Cut off from the frantic gold rush, the park area became home to ranching, farming, logging, and quartz mining.

In 1960, the first piece of land was purchased to establish Golden Gate Canyon State Park. Other land purchases were to follow, eventually totaling more than 14,000 acres.

Facilities & Activities

There are more than 275 scenic picnic sites located along Ralston Creek, at Ole' Barn Knoll, Bootleg Bottom, Panorama Point and Kriley and Slough ponds. Groups of up to 150 can reserve the Red Barn Group Picnic area. The area provides barrier-free access to covered picnic tables, stand-up grills, vault toilets, and a volleyball court.

Weddings: Up to 40 people are allowed and scheduled at Panorama Point Scenic Overlook and picnic area. The area consists of a large wooden deck that overlooks the Continental Divide. For scheduling information call the park office at ☎ (303) 592-1502.

Fishing: Permitted in any stream or pond in the park except the Visitors Center show pond. Ralston Creek and all of the ponds are stocked regularly by the Colorado Division of Wildlife. A Colorado fishing license (available at the Visitors Center) is required and Division of Wildlife regulations apply.

Hunting: Permitted in the Jefferson County portion of the park only. No hunting is allowed from the Friday prior to Memorial Day until the Tuesday following Labor Day. Information on seasons and regulations is available at the park office.

Hiking: Nearly 35 miles of hiking trails in the park offer opportunities and challenges for everyone. The 12 trails are each named for an animal native to the area and are marked with the animal's footprint. The difficulty of the trail is indicated by the background shape of the footprint marker. Trailheads with parking areas are easily accessible from the main roads in the park. Horseback riding is allowed on any easy-rated trail.

Camping: The 106-site Reverend's Ridge Campground accommodates trailers, pick-up campers and tents, and offers flush toilets, hot showers, and laundry facilities. During the summer months, campfire programs are presented in an outdoor amphitheater.

Aspen Meadow Campground provides 35 campsites for tents only. Facilities include water pumps, vault toilets, and fire rings. Rimrock Loop at Aspen Meadow has camping sites and parking designed for horseback riders.

For those who want a more primitive and somewhat unusual camping experience, there are four back country shelters available at Golden Gate. These three-sided structures, with a roof and wooden floor, are built in the Appalachian trail-hut tradition and can sleep up to six people eliminating the need for a tent. In addition to the shelters, there are 23 back country tent sites. Back country camping permits must be obtained at the Visitor's Center. No fires are allowed in the back country.

Winter Activities: Golden Gate offers year-round recreational activities. For peace and solitude, winter is an excellent time to visit. Opportunities abound for cross-country skiing, snowshoeing, ice fishing and skating, winter hiking or camping, sledding, tubing, and photography. A winter guide is available at the Visitors Center. Winter enthusiasts are encouraged to call the park office for current conditions, ☎ (303) 592-1502.

For further information contact: Park Superintendent, Golden Gate State Park, Route C Box 280, Golden, CO 80403. ☎ (303) 592-1502.

Harvey Gap State Park

Location: Five miles east of Rifle Gap Reservoir.

Known for its premier windsurfing, Harvey Gap also offers hiking, boating, and picnicking. In the winter, visitors can snowmobile, cross-country ski, and ice fish.

Administered by the Colorado Division of Parks and Outdoor Recreation, this day-use-only area sits at an elevation of 6,100 feet. Harvey Gap State Park is a beautiful cedar and sagebrush biome, with a grand hogback – a mountain ridge that runs along the backside of the park.

The original earthen dam at Harvey Gap reservoir was constructed in 1890. That dam broke and was replaced by the existing one around 1902.

Primarily used to irrigate the surrounding region, Harvey Gap also provides a haven for the recreationist.

Camping: Camping is not allowed here, but is permitted at Rifle Gapand Rifle Falls state parks – a short drive from Harvey Gap.

Picnicking: Harvey Gap maintains 30 picnic sites with grills. Some line the reservoir, while others sit on an overlook above the lake.

Water Recreation: Boating (20 H.P. or less motors), swimming, diving, sailing, and windsurfing are popular.

Fishing: Bass fishing is some of the best around during the summer. Fishermen can also snare catfish and crappie here. Wintertime offers rainbow trout for the avid angler.

Hunting: Small game and waterfowl are most popular during hunting season. There is excellent big game hunting in the White River National Forest and on lands administered by the US Bureau of Land Management, both near the park. Information on seasons and regulations is available from any park ranger.

Winter Recreation: Cold weather enthusiasts come to Harvey Gap to cross-country ski, ice fish, and to snowmobile.

Harvey Gap State Park

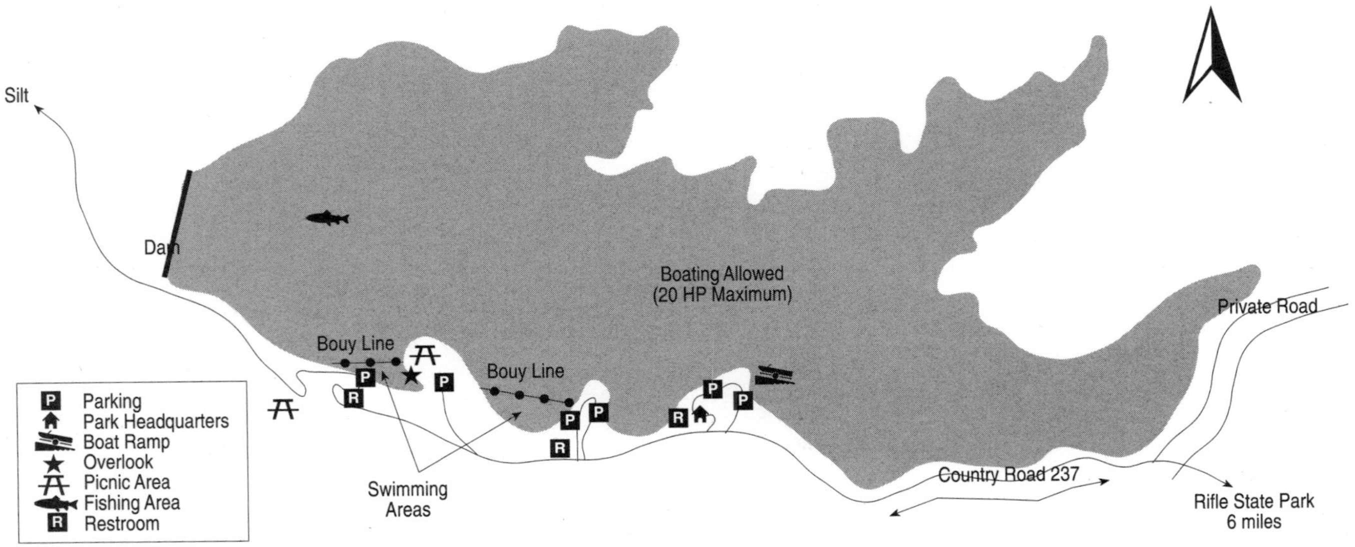

N

Private Road

Rifle State Park
6 miles

Country Road 237

Boating Allowed
(20 HP Maximum)

Bouy Line

Bouy Line

Swimming
Areas

Silt

Dam

Legend

- **P** Parking
- Park Headquarters
- Boat Ramp
- ★ Overlook
- 开 Picnic Area
- Fishing Area
- **R** Restroom

Community Facilities: All commercial, medical, and religious facilities are available in Rifle, approximately 15 miles from Harvey Gap.

For further information contact: Park Superintendent, Harvey Gap State Park, c/o Rifle Gap State Park, 0050 County Road 219, Rifle, CO 81650. ☎ (303) 625-1607.

Highline State Park

Location: Seven miles NW of Loma near Highway 139.

Highline State Park provides a comfortable setting for waterskiing, swimming, fishing, and picnicking. Highline Lake, completed in 1969, has 160 surface acres for water recreation, while Mack Mesa Lake provides good fishing and an escape from motorized boats. In winter, large numbers of migratory birds use the park as a rest stop. Whether you visit Highline to rest or play, its diverse wildlife and recreational opportunities will entertain you.

Camping: Highline State Park offers 25 grassy campsites that accommodate both tents and RVs. Showers are available. Campers must have both a camping permit and a parks pass, both available at the park entrance.

Fishing: Mack Mesa Lake is noted for its fine early-season trout fishing. Only hand or electric powered boats are allowed.

Highline Lake has good warm-water fishing, especially for catfish and crappie.

Wildlife: More than 150 species of birds have been observed at Highline State Park. Migrating ducks and geese winter at Highline Lake. Birds such as the great blue heron, white pelican, snowy egret, whooping crane, golden eagle, and bald eagle are seen in the park.

Many small animals make their home at Highline, and natural areas within the park allow visitors and school groups to observe animals in their natural habitats.

Highline State Park

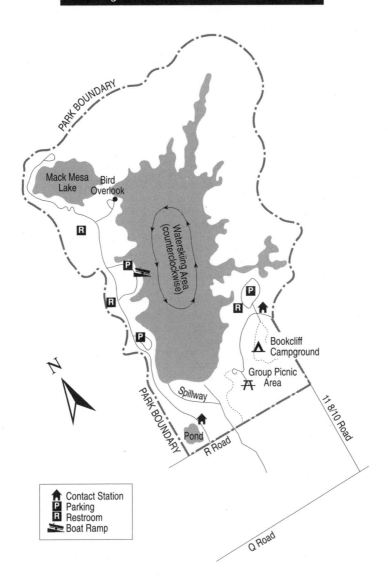

PARK BOUNDARY

Mack Mesa Lake

Bird Overlook

Waterskiing Area (counterclockwise)

R

P

R

P

R

P

Bookcliff Campground

Group Picnic Area

Spillway

PARK BOUNDARY

Pond

R Road

11 8/10 Road

Q Road

N

Contact Station
P Parking
R Restroom
Boat Ramp

Hunting at Highline State Park is controlled. Information on seasons and regulations is available from any park ranger or the local Division of Wildlife office (☎ 970-248-7175).

Boating/Water Recreation: Highline Lake is well-known as a fine boating and waterskiing area. Boaters must obey Colorado boating statutes and regulations, which are available in pamphlet form at the entrance station.

Park rangers patrol Highline regularly to provide emergency assistance, carry out boat safety inspections, and ensure safe operation of crafts on the lakes within the park.

A swimming area is located on the southeast shore of Highline Lake near the dam, although no lifeguard is provided.

For further information contact: Park Superintendent, Highline State Park, 1800 11.8 Road, Loma, CO 81524. ☎ (970) 858-7208.

Jackson Lake State Park

Location: 80 miles NE of Denver and 20 miles NW of Ft. Morgan on I-76.

*O*nce known primarily for the hunting around its banks, Jackson Lake State Park has become one of Colorado's finest outdoor recreation and water sports sites. The area is known for its shoreline camping and its large, warm-water reservoir with sandy bottom and beaches. For fun in the sun and unlimited recreational opportunities, Jackson Lake is the place.

Besides providing a wide variety of outdoor recreation opportunities, the 2,700 surface-acre lake is an important irrigation reservoir that holds water for the thousands of acres of Colorado farmland to the south and east. The reservoir was built at the turn of the century and encompasses an existing lake. The surrounding park covers 440 acres.

Picnicking: Jackson Lake has 60 picnic sites and a group picnic area is available by reservation through the park office.

Water Sports: All areas of Jackson Lake are open to waterskiing. Boats towing skiers must stay 150 feet from the swim area, moored vessels, the concrete dike, and shore fishermen. Both an observer and an operator must be in any boat that is towing a skier. Ski counter-clockwise, and please avoid dangerous congestion.

Jackson Lake's sandy beaches and gradually sloping lake bottom make it ideal for swimming, which is allowed in the two designated swimming areas only. Swimming is entirely at the individual's own risk.

Boating: A boat ramp is located on the west shore of the lake. All boats must comply with current Colorado boating statutes and regulations available in pamphlet form at the entrance stations and boat ramp. No boats are allowed in or near the beaches, outlet tube area, inlet, or dike fishing area. The lake is closed to motorized boating from November 1 through the first spring day that ALL ice is off the reservoir.

Camping: Jackson Lake State Park has 262 campsites. Most accommodate campers or trailers and tents. Facilities include showers, toilets, laundry, electric hookups, and drinking water. Quiet hours are observed from 10 PM to 6 AM. Camping permits expire at noon. If a site is not renewed by noon, it is considered available to be reassigned to another camper.

Fishing: Jackson Lake is home to trout, walleye, bass, catfish, perch, crappie, and wipers. The lake has become a popular spot for anglers. Fishing is restricted during waterfowl hunting season and is prohibited from the beaches year-round.

Hunting/Wildlife: Hunters come to Jackson Lake State Park for waterfowl, dove, pheasant, and rabbits. Hunting in the park is controlled and permitted from the Tuesday after Labor Day through the Friday prior to Memorial Day. Only bow and arrows and shotguns loaded with birdshot are allowed. Waterfowl hunters must use steel shot.

An abundance of wildlife can be observed and photographed in the park. The list includes pelicans, eagles, hawks, heron, deer, coyote, waterfowl, and numerous shore birds.

Winter Recreation: During the winter months, Jackson Lake State Park offers camping, wildlife observation, photography, ice boating, ice fishing, and ice skating. Please check with a ranger for weather and ice conditions.

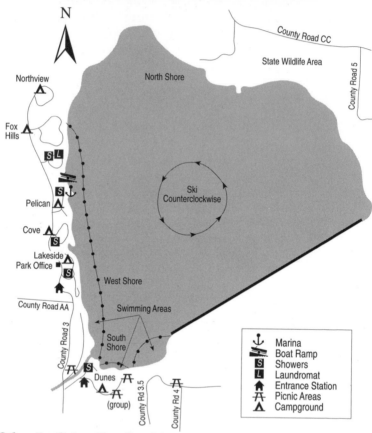

Other Facilities: Shoreline Marina provides food and drink, boat rentals, boat launching services, boat storage, boat wash, gas, boating, fishing, camping, and picnic supplies. The amphitheater in Cove Campground offers weekend interpretive programs Memorial Day through Labor Day.

For further information contact: Park Superintendent, Jackson Lake State Park, #26363 Road 3, Orchard, CO 80649. ☎ (970) 645-2551.

Lathrop State Park

Location: Just off of County Rd. 502 in Walsenburg.

Lathrop State Park lies on a high plains grassland dotted with pinon and juniper that is typical of southeastern Colorado. Visitors may see mule deer, rabbits, squirrels, and a variety of birds and waterfowl hidden among the yucca. The park is a popular place to enjoy fishing, sailing, windsurfing, swimming, camping, and hiking.

The Spanish Peaks, 13,610 and 12,669 ft. in elevation, tower over the southern end of the park and attract visitors with their majestic beauty, geological interest, and historical legends. The peaks were used for many years as directional guides by trappers, prospectors, settlers, and explorers. The plains Indians named the peaks Huajatolla (Wa-ha-toy-a), which means "the twins."

The area surrounding the Spanish Peaks, the Valley of the Rising Sun, was believed by the Indians to be a strange, mysterious place inhabited by the gods of many lost tribes. Legends tell of great lost gold mines and a "garden of paradise" at the base of the Huajatollas. The Indians used the mined gold only for worship, but some gold was taken to Mexico for coinage. The gods, angry at this, placed a demon in the peaks to bring bad luck or death to anyone who mines gold there.

With the assistance of Huerfano County residents, Lathrop was leased in 1962 as Colorado's first state park. It is named for the first director of the Division of Parks and Outdoor Recreation, Harold W. Lathrop.

Martin Lake offers a beach, waterskiing, fishing, power-and sailboating, and windsurfing. Swimming is permitted only in desig nated areas and is at the individual's own risk. The lake is divided into zones by buoys that designate a limited or specialized activity on the lake. Please review the zoning system posted at the boat ramp. Horseshoe Lake offers sailing, boating at wakeless speeds, fishing, and windsurfing.

In addition, waterski boats must have an observer on board with the driver. A red 12" x 12" flag must be displayed when a skier is down in the water. If you have any questions about equipment requirements, please contact a park ranger.

Lathrop State Park has 96 campsites and two group camping areas. The campgrounds accommodate motor homes, trailers, and tents, and offer both primitive and modern camping experiences. Dump stations and water hydrants are available throughout both campgrounds. Trash receptacles are provided in common areas in both campgrounds.

Yucca Campground has 17 sites plus two group camping areas and provides a primitive camping experience with gravel pull-in spaces and vault toilets. Pinon Campground has 79 sites and features pull-through paved sites, electrical hook-ups, flush toilets, laundry facilities, a shower house, a playground, and access to the amphitheater.

Martin and Horseshoe lakes are stocked with rainbow trout, channel catfish, tiger musky bass, walleye, bluegill, and crappie. Fishing is enjoyed all year, including ice fishing in the winter. A fishing area for children under 15 years of age is located near the Martin Lake Dam. The beach, boat dock, and boat ramps are closed to fishing.

Fishing licenses are required for everyone over fourteen years of age.

Only the posted areas around Horseshoe Lake are open for water-fowl and small game hunting during regular seasons. Only shot-guns and bows and arrows are permitted during open seasons. Hunting licenses are required.

Walsenburg Golf Club

Walsenburg Golf Club is open to the public. This beautiful nine-hole golf course is adjacent to the park and overlooks Martin Lake and the Spanish Peaks. It is within walking distance of Pinon Campground. The spacious clubhouse features a restaurant, lounge, and pro shop.

Unique in its conception, this city/county golf course is the result of 50 independent businessmen and professionals dedicated to building and maintaining this all-grass course with elevated greens. The club is managed by Orlando Herrera.

For further information contact: Park Superintendent, Lathrop State Park, 70 County Road 502, Walsenburg, CO 81089. ☎ (719) 738-2376.

Mancos Lake State Park

Location: 10 miles from Mesa Verde National Monument in SW Colorado.

Situated at an elevation of 7,800 ft. on the scenic new San Juan Skyway, Mancos State Park is surrounded by the majestic San Juan mountain range. The area has more 300 land acres and the reservoir, which was once called Jackson Gulch, provides 216 surface acres of water for recreation.

Jackson Gulch Dam at Mancos Lake was constructed in 1948 by the Bureau of Reclamation in conjunction with the Young Adult Conservation Corps. It supplies the drinking water for Mesa Verde and the surrounding rural areas.

Mancos Lake State Park

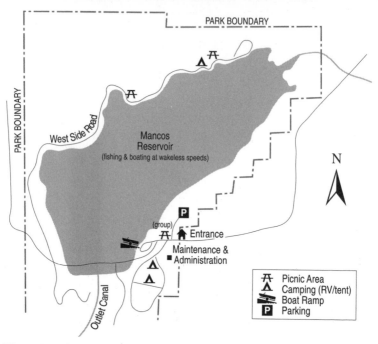

There is a beautiful campground here, nestled within a mature ponderosa pine forest. Wakeless boating and excellent year-round fishing await the recreationist looking for a relaxing day. Picnickers and hikers will find pleasing sites and trails.

Mancos State Park is managed by the Colorado Division of Parks and Outdoor Recreation, in cooperation with the US Bureau of Reclamation and the Mancos Water Conservancy District.

The pleasant climate and many diversions make Mancos a not-to-be-missed stop on your next trip through southwestern Colorado.

Boating: Boaters must observe the Colorado boating statutes and regulations, which are available at the park entrance. Only wakeless boating is permitted at Mancos Lake. No waterskiing or swimming is allowed.

Camping: Mancos State Park has 24 campsites, most located on the south side of the reservoir in a mature ponderosa pine forest. There are vault toilets and drinking water but no electrical hookups.

Along the northwest side of the reservoir, there are nine campsites, primarily for tent campers. There are toilets but no drinking water nearby. Check-out time is noon. A dump station is located at the exit leaving the campground.

Hiking/Nature Trails: A four-mile trail weaves through Mancos, meeting Chicken Creek Trail which connects with a network of trails on US Forestland. The trail system is for hiking, horseback riding, and mountain bikes. Mancos State Park now has a trailhead connected to the Durango and Denver, Colorado Trail.

Winter Recreation: Cold weather enthusiasts can cross-country ski, snowmobile, and ice fish at Mancos Lake.

Wildlife: Deer, elk, small game animals, migrating bald eagles and waterfowl, hawks, raptors, and hummingbirds are among the wildlife seen at Mancos.

Community Facilities: Gas and groceries can be obtained in Mancos, five miles from the park.

For further information contact: Park Superintendent, Mancos Lake State Park, c/o Navajo State Park, Box 1697, Arboles, CO 80814. ☎ (303) 883-2208. Summer Season Only: ☎ (303) 533-7065.

Mueller State Park

Location: In Teller County just west of Divide, Colorado.

The park is a wildlife habitat shared by elk, big horn sheep, mule deer, eagles, hawks, and a variety of small mammals and song birds. In remote areas, bears, bobcats, and mountain lions are able to live in freedom. The park supports a myriad of plant-life species. Calypso orchards and soft ferns to wiry prairie grasses and tenacious ground cover plants grow throughout. Stands of spruce, fir pine, juniper and aspen flourish in their own micro climates.

The park's topography varies from rolling timber and grassland interrupted by dramatic rock outcroppings in the north, to the south portion of the park where rugged terrain hosts Fourmile Creek, Sheep Nose, and the impressive Dome Rock. This contrast results from an ancient up-thrust of Pikes Peak to the east and volcanic action to the west.

Once hunting grounds of the Ute Indians, the land was settled by pioneers in the 1860s. Prospectors trampled through the land to Cripple Creek and Victor during the gold rush. Lumber was harvested for nearby towns, mines, and railroads. Cattle grazing and farming were occasionally supplemented by boot-legging, horse thievery, and cattle-rustling.

The former owners, the Mueller Family, designated their cattle ranch as a game preserve. Today resident elk and big horn sheep flourish as a result of this protection.

Today, visitors enjoy year-round recreational opportunities including camping, picnicking, trail use, fishing, and nature studies. Winter activities include ice skating, snowshoeing, and ski touring. Every season is a photographers delight. The park is administered by Colorado State Parks in cooperation with the Colorado Division of Wildlife.

Picnicking: Forty-one scenic picnic areas are located in four day-use areas. Facilities include grills, tables, drinking water, and restrooms.

Camping: The campground is located in a forest setting of spruce, fir, and aspen with panoramic views of the Rocky Mountains. The park has 90 sites, including 12 walk-in tent sites and a reservable group campground. The campground can accommodate motor-homes, trailers, and tents. A camper services facility is centrally located in the campground with modern restrooms, hot showers, and laundry facilities. All sites, except the walk-in tent sites, have electric hookups, and drinking water is available. There are no sewer hookups, but a dump station is available.

Campers are limited to one camping unit and a maximum of six persons per site.

Trails: Nearly 90 miles of trails invite visitors to explore the park's natural and historical resources. Trails vary from short, leisurely walks to challenging, full-day hikes. Most trails are open to hikers and cyclists, with a few ecologically fragile areas restricted to hikers only. Some larger loop trails are designated for horseback riders. An ample horse-trailer parking and unloading area is provided. Winter ski touring and snowshoeing can be enjoyed on a

Mueller State Park & Wildlife Area

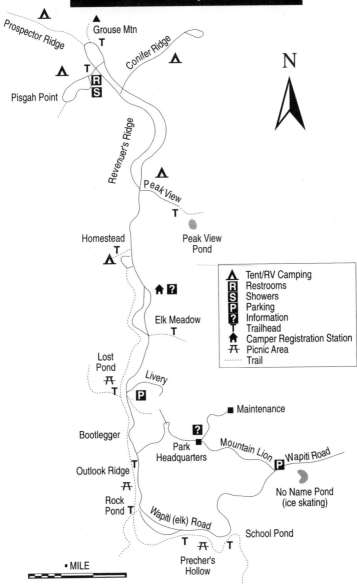

Prospector Ridge

Grouse Mtn
T

Conifer Ridge

Pisgah Point
T
R
S

N

Revenuer's Ridge

Peak View
T

Homestead
T

Peak View Pond

Tent/RV Camping
R **Restrooms**
S **Showers**
P **Parking**
? **Information**
T **Trailhead**
🏠 **Camper Registration Station**
🎋 **Picnic Area**
---- **Trail**

Elk Meadow
T

Lost Pond
T

Livery

P

■ Maintenance

?

Park Headquarters

Bootlegger

Mountain Lion

Wapiti Road

P

Outlook Ridge

No Name Pond
(ice skating)

Rock Pond T

Wapiti (elk) Road

School Pond

• MILE

T   T

Precher's Hollow

variety of terrain. There are 50 trails in the park. Each trail is named and numbered. Hikers should use established and marked trails. Trailhead and parking areas are easily accessible from the main roads in the park. Trail maps are available at park headquarters.

Fishing/Hunting: Anglers can fish Fourmile Creek and a few of the ponds in the park. They are stocked with trout by the Division of Wildlife. A Colorado fishing license is required, and Division of Wildlife regulations apply. Fishing with ties and lures is encouraged. If you return fish to the water put them back alive. Hunting is limited and controlled. Information on seasons and regulations is available from park rangers and the park Headquarters. The use of firearms is prohibited during the summer and controlled during legal hunting seasons.

For further information contact: Park Superintendent, Mueller State Park and Wildlife Area, PO Box 49, Divide, CO 80814. ☎ (719) 687-2366.

Navajo State Park

Location: Outside Arboles, 35 miles south of Pagosa Springs, 45 miles southeast of Durango.

The park's main attraction is the 35-mile-long Navajo Reservoir, which extends well into New Mexico. The 15,000 acres, including 3,000 acres on the Colorado side, offer a challenge to the angler and unlimited pleasure to the boater and waterskier. Navajo boasts Colorado's largest boat ramp – 80' wide, a quarter mile long – and a good recreational airstrip, used frequently by flying buffs and fly-in campers.

History: The visitor center museum echoes the way of life of the ancient people of the area. Hikers get a feeling of the past as they follow an old stagecoach road or an abandoned railroad bed.

The Navajo Dam in New Mexico was constructed by the US Bureau of Reclamation in 1962. In Colorado, the Division of Parks and Outdoor Recreation administers the area, which has been managed by the state since 1964.

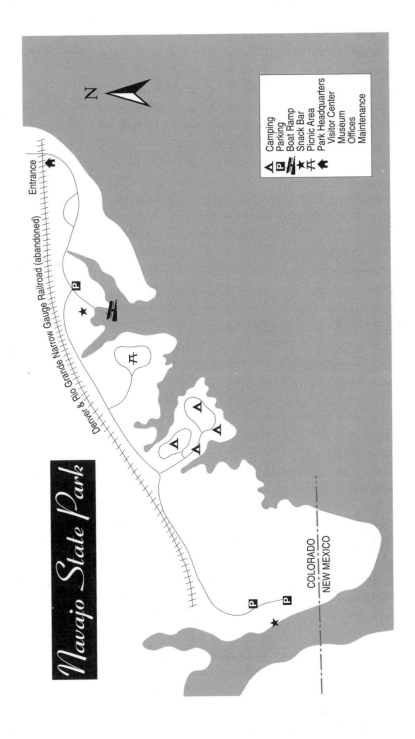

Navajo State Park

N

Entrance

Denver & Rio Grande Narrow Gauge Railroad (abandoned)

COLORADO
NEW MEXICO

▲ Camping
🅿 Parking
🚤 Boat Ramp
★ Snack Bar
🛖 Picnic Area
🔦 Park Headquarters
　 Visitor Center
　 Museum
　 Offices
　 Maintenance

Camping: Navajo's modern campground offers 70 sites, showers and flush toilets. Many sites have pull-throughs, all can accommodate tents, trailers, or pick-up campers. Please camp only in designated sites and display your camping permit in the marker at your campsite. The campground is patrolled for your safety. Quiet after 10 PM.

Boating: Water sports are the principal activities at Navajo State Park. Boaters are subject to Colorado boating statutes and regulations, available at the entrance station. New Mexico laws and regulations apply to boaters who cross the state line. The two states have a reciprocal arrangement honoring current boat registrations and inspection stickers.

Fishing: Bluegill, catfish, crappie, and largemouth bass lie in the shallows and near the lake surface. Kokanee salmon and many varieties of trout are found in the deeps.

Roads off Highway 151 and County Road 557 to Pagosa Junction give access to good fishing spots on the Piedra and San Juan rivers. Fishing condition reports are available at the visitor center. Visitors planning to fish in New Mexico's waters as well as Colorado's must have fishing licenses from both states.

Wildlife/Hunting: Waterfowl, shorebirds, birds of prey, including the bald eagle, and such songbirds as waxwings, thrushes, and meadowlarks are found at Navajo along with game birds like doves, grouse, and turkeys. Visitors may also see beaver, mink, foxes, deer, elk, rabbits and, in the remote areas, coyotes, bobcats, or lions.

Deer, elk, and bird hunting are allowed here in established seasons. Check with the park office for information.

Airfield: 3,150', N/S dirt runway, 75' wide. Listed in the FAA Airport Master Record. Tie-downs for nine aircrafts are provided; no landing fee.

Nature Study & Museum: Featured at the Visitor Center are changing exhibits of Indian artifacts excavated from areas now submerged beneath Navajo Reservoir. The site was populated by the Anasazi until the 14th century when the ancestors of the modern Ute and Navajo tribes moved in from the north.

Winter Recreation: Snowmobiling, ski touring, snowshoeing, ice fishing, open water fishing, and boating.

Other Facilities: A marina provides gas, boat repairs, food service, and groceries. Slip and buoy rental is available as well as fishing and skiing gear. Open March through November.

For further information contact: Park Superintendent, Navajo State Park, Box 1697, Arboles, CO 81121. ☎ (303) 883-2208.

North Sterling State Park

Location: In Sterling on County Road 330.

M ajestic bluffs and expansive views of the high plains greeted early settlers traveling the nearby Overland Trail. Those panoramic views now welcome visitors to one of Colorado's newest state parks, North Sterling State Park.

North Sterling Reservoir is a boater's paradise, offering a 3,000-acre lake with an interesting array of coves and fingers to explore. An additional 1,000 acres of land incorporates modern facilities and supports a wide variety of recreational activities. The surrounding area is home to a diversity of wildlife and has a rich historical heritage.

Built at the turn of the century, the reservoir serves as an important irrigation facility for the lower South Platte River Valley. Colorado State Parks acquired the area in 1992 and manages recreation on the reservoir through a perpetual easement with North Sterling Irrigation District.

Facilities & Access: The marina concession is located on the northeast corner of the reservoir, and offers a full range of products and services. Public boat ramps on North Sterling Reservoir are located at Elks Campground, Balanced Rock and Hilltop Point.

Public access is limited to the surface roads of the reservoir and state-owned land. Please respect private property boundaries and stay within designated areas.

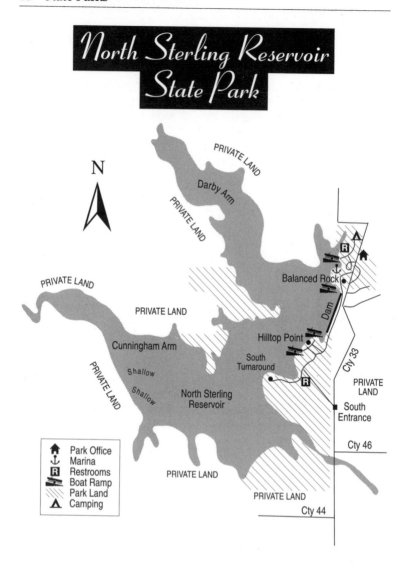

Camping: The Elks Campground can accommodate recreational vehicles, trailers, or tents. Individual hookups are not yet available at the park. Campers are limited to one camping unit per site and a maximum of six people per site.

Dispersed camping is permitted south of the Dam, by permit only, in areas not posted against such use. Dispersed camping will be discontinued when new camping facilities are constructed on the south side.

Fishing: The reservoir is an excellent warm-water fishery featuring walleye, crappie, perch, bass, bluegill, catfish, and wiper.

North Sterling Reservoir is open to fishing year-round. Ice fishing is permitted during the migratory waterfowl hunting season, as conditions allow.

Winter Recreation: North Sterling Reservoir State Park is open daily, year-round. During the winter months, the park offers camping, hunting, ice fishing, and opportunities for photography and wildlife observation. Snowmobiling is not permitted.

Boating/Waterskiing: Boaters must observe the Colorado boating statutes and regulations, available in pamphlet form at the park office and entrances. Boats are required to maintain a wakeless speed around launch facilities, within 150 ft. of shore fishermen, and other areas as marked. waterskiers must ski in a counterclockwise direction. Each ski boat needs an observer on board, in addition to the operator. A 12" x 12" red flag must be displayed whenever a skier is down or equipment is in the water.

The water level at North Sterling Reservoir fluctuates during the irrigation season. Boaters should be especially alert to submerged hazards. The reservoir is closed to boating each year on November 1, through the end of the migratory waterfowl hunting season.

Wildlife: A wide variety of wildlife may be found in the area, including deer, eagles, pelicans, coyotes, rabbits and many species of waterfowl and shorebirds.

Hunting: Carefully managed and permitted during established seasons from the first Tuesday after Labor Day through the Friday before Memorial Day. Methods of hunting are restricted to bows and arrows and shotguns loaded with birdshot. Hunting is not permitted from the dam.

For further information contact: Park Superintendent, North Sterling Reservoir State Park, 24006 County Road 330, Sterling, CO 80751. ☎ (970) 522-3657.

Paonia State Park

Location:Approximately 16 miles NE of the town of Paonia on State Highway 133. From Glenwood Springs, travel nine miles on Highway 82 to Carbondale, turn south on Highway 133 and travel 44 miles.

Situated in the shadow of the majestic Ragged Mountain, Paonia State Park, with an elevation of 6,500 ft., is a popular place for camping, picnicking, waterskiing, fishing, boating, and outdoor photography.

Paonia offers 15 campsites, vault toilets, and a concrete boat ramp. There is no drinking water available, so bring your own.

Paonia State Park is surrounded by the Gunnison National Forest and spectacular mountain scenery Camping, sightseeing, and picnicking are possible activities here.

Camping: Paonia State Park has 15 campsites, located in two separate campgrounds. Spruce campground, located next to Highway 133, offers eight campsites in a scenic setting with towering blue spruce trees and a babbling stream a few feet away. Hawsapple campground, situated across the river, is popular with waterskiers. All campsites have a picnic table, a fire ring, and vault toilets are nearby. Campers are charged $6 per night, and each vehicle must have a valid park pass. Please note that no drinking water is available in the park.

Boating: All boaters must observe the current Colorado boating statutes and regulations. All motorboats and sailboards must have the current year registration. Boating activities include waterskiing, jet skiing, boat fishing, and general recreation.

Fishing: Some northern pike and rainbow trout can be caught in the reservoir from late June until late August. The best fishing is fly-fishing the confluence of the Muddy Creek and the Anthracite Creek below the dam.

Wildlife: Chipmunks, squirrels, rabbits, and other small mammals abound throughout the park. Paonia State Park is a popular place to spot all types of birds. Visitors may also see an occasional mule deer, elk, or even a black bear.

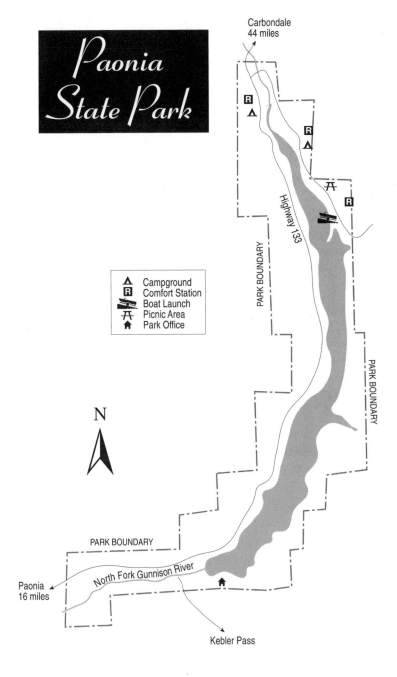

Carbondale
44 miles

R

R

Highway 133

R

PARK BOUNDARY

Campground
Comfort Station
Boat Launch
Picnic Area
Park Office

PARK BOUNDARY

N

PARK BOUNDARY

North Fork Gunnison River

Paonia
16 miles

Kebler Pass

For further information contact: Park Superintendent, Paonia State Park, c/o Crawford State Park, Box 147, Crawford, CO 81415. ☎ (303) 921-5721.

Spinney Mountain State Park

Location: From Colorado Springs take Highway 24 west for 55 miles. Turn left on park County Road 23, go 2.8 miles. Turn right on County Road 59 and go 1.1 miles to the park entrance. Or, Spinney Mountain State Park is 7 miles west of Eleven Mile State Park off County Road 59.

Spinney Mountain State Park is nestled in the southeast corner of South Park at the foot of Spinney Mountain to the north and 39-Mile Mountain to the south. With spectacular views of the acclaimed Collegiate Mountain Range to the west and south, the park is an isolated retreat. Thanks to its 2,500 acre reservoir and its prime location along the South Platte River, the park offers exceptional boating, picnicking, and waterfowl hunting, but its prized attraction is nationally renowned fishing.

The delicate ecosystem is very sensitive to man. Wildflowers are rampant and deer, coyote, raccoon, and antelope roam the region. Ducks, Canadian geese, grebes, rails, and pelicans are common. Bald and golden eagles make cameo appearances in the park.

The park is a day-use area only, opening 30 minutes before sunrise and closing one hour after sunset. Built in 1982, its season lasts from approximately May 1 to November 15.

Fishing: Spinney Mountain is a trophy and designated gold medal water fishery.

In 1982, before the park was officially opened, the waters were stocked with Snake River cutthroat trout. Today, the area is home to trophy-size cutthroats, as well as northern pike, rainbow, and brown trout.

Anglers may keep only one trout, which must be 20 inches in length or longer. All northern pike caught between 26 and 34 inches in length must be returned to the water immediately. The bag and possession limit for northern pike is 10, of which no more than one can be greater than 34 inches in length.

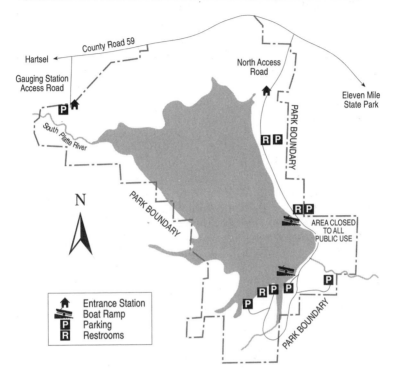

Only artificial flies and lures are permitted. Bait fishing and snagging are prohibited.

The area within the fence below the dam and the Homestake Diversion Channel are closed to fishing.

Picnicking: Picnicking is allowed anywhere in the park. Spinney offers several picnic areas with tables and fire rings. Fires must be within the rings.

Hunting: Waterfowl, small game, and varmints can be hunted at Spinney. Hunting is allowed during lawful seasons in areas not posted as no hunting.

Facilities: Commercial and religious facilities are available in the town of Hartsel, 10 miles west of the north entrance or in Lake George, 19 miles to the east.

For further information contact: Park Superintendent, Spinney Mountain State Park, 4229 County Road 92, Lake George, CO 80827-4229. ☎ (719) 748-3401.

Stagecoach State Park

Location: On Country Road 14 on the way to Oak Creek.

*W*agon wheels and ore cars are two symbols of the area's rich history Stagecoaches traveled over Yellow Jacket Pass, now County Road 14, on their way to Oak Creek or Steamboat Springs. The fertile upper Yampa Valley attracted early ranchers, farmers and coal miners. Many of the reservoir's campgrounds and picnic areas are named after early coal mines and mining camps. The valley also attracted land developers, who visualized a resort community in the area. Today, visitors to Stagecoach Reservoir enjoy a variety of recreational activities.

Located in the lower elevation of the river valley, native grasses, shrubs, and flowering plants are the dominant vegetation. Visitors enjoy views of the Flattop Mountains to the southwest, and to the north, the cliff face of Blacktail Mountain.

Built as a water storage facility by the Upper Yampa Water Conservancy District, three-mile-long Stagecoach Reservoir is a new addition to the state park system. The Colorado Division of Parks and Outdoor Recreation manages the recreational uses of the reservoir under a lease with the water district.

Fishing: The reservoir is known for its fast-growing, hard-fighting rainbows and the occasional brown or brook trout and Snake River cutthroat. The reservoir is also stocked with northern pike and kokanee salmon. Special regulations apply in the Yampa River below the dam, so please review the current Colorado fishing regulations. Brochures are available at the entrance station or park office.

Camping: The park's Junction City, Pinnacle, Harding Spur, and McKinley campgrounds have a total of 92 campsites, which can accommodate tents, campers, or trailers. One handicapped accessible campsite is available. Junction City and Pinnacle camp-

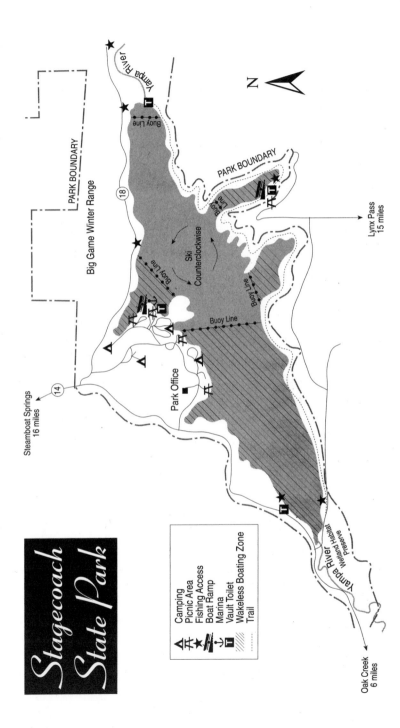

Stagecoach State Park

Legend:
- Camping
- Picnic Area
- Fishing Access
- Boat Ramp
- Marina
- Vault Toilet
- Wakeless Boating Zone
- Trail

N

PARK BOUNDARY

Big Game Winter Range

PARK BOUNDARY

Yampa River

Buoy Line

Ski Counterclockwise

Buoy Line

Buoy Line

Buoy Line

Park Office

Yampa River Wetland Habitat Preserve

18

14

Steamboat Springs 16 miles

Lynx Pass 15 miles

Oak Creek 6 miles

grounds have pull-through sites and electrical hookups. Only one camping unit per site is allowed.

Campground users must have both a camping permit and park pass. Please display camping permits in the plastic holder at the campsite.

Reservations: Reservations can be made a minimum of three days and a maximum of 90 days in advance. You may reserve up to six sites per call. (If you're paying by check, the three-day minimum doesn't apply; your reservation must be made a minimum of 14 days in advance.)

Picnicking: Picnicking is popular at the park and facilities are located at the South Shore boat ramp, Arrowhead, Keystone, and Haybro picnic areas. Each site has a picnic table and standing grill. Arrowhead group area is available for groups of up to 100 on a reservation basis only. Call the park office, ☎ (970) 736-2436, to reserve this area.

Trails: Located on the south side of the reservoir is a five-mile non-motorized trail.

Boating/Water Sports: Stagecoach Reservoir hosts a variety of water sports. Boaters are subject to current Colorado boating statutes and regulations, available in pamphlet form at the entrance station or park office. A boat ramp is located at the marina near Pinnacle Campground and at the Morrison Cove area.

Waterskiing is permitted only in designated areas of the reservoir. Boats towing skiers must keep 150 ft. from shore and must have an observer on board in addition to the operator. Ski patterns are counterclockwise.

Swimming is allowed only in the designated area, located near Pinnacle Campground.

Other facilities include a marina concession which provides boat rentals, fishing, and camping supplies.

Wildlife/Hunting: Elk, mule deer, badger, raccoon, muskrat, squirrels, and chipmunks inhabit the area. A large variety of birds are found in the park, including sage grouse, hawks, eagles, various songbirds, and waterfowl. The use of firearms and other weapons are prohibited in the summer and controlled during the legal hunting seasons. Information on the seasons and regulations are available from the park staff.

Winter Recreation: During the winter, visitors can enjoy ice fishing, cross-country skiing, and snowmobiling. Snowmobiling is allowed only in designated areas. The west entrance provides access into the park during the winter. The Keystone parking area is plowed and available for day-use and limited winter camping. There is a vault toilet available at Keystone.

For further information contact: Park Superintendent, Stagecoach State Park, PO Box 98, Oak Creek, CO 80467. ☎ (970) 736-2436.

Steamboat & Pearl Lake State Park

Location: Take US 40 west from Steamboat Springs for two miles to County Road 129. Turn north and continue 26 miles to the Steamboat Lake Park. Pearl Lake's entrance is three miles south of the turnoff to Steamboat Lake Park.

*N*estled in a valley at the foot of majestic Hahn's Peak, only a few miles west of the Continental Divide, Steamboat Lake State Park offers its visitors one of the most beautiful settings in Colorado, no matter what the season. The park is famed for water sports and fishing. Routt National Forest is adjacent to the park, providing additional recreational opportunities, while the bright lights of Steamboat Springs are only 27 miles away for visitors who want an occasional night on the town.

Two sparkling man-made lakes – Steamboat and Pearl – are principle features of the 1,550-acre park. Steamboat Lake (1,053 acres) was completed in 1968. Pearl Lake (190 acres), completed in 1962, is named in honor of Mrs. Pearl Hartt, who was instrumental in aiding the state's land acquisition for construction of the lake. A local resident, Mrs. Hartt was one of the many in a community who helped to make the State Park a reality.

A survey of Colorado park rangers revealed that Steamboat Lake is their favorite vacation spot. One visit to this remarkable area and you will see why!

Camping: The park's Sunrise Vista, Dutch Hill, and Pearl Lake campgrounds have 222 campsites between them, accommodating

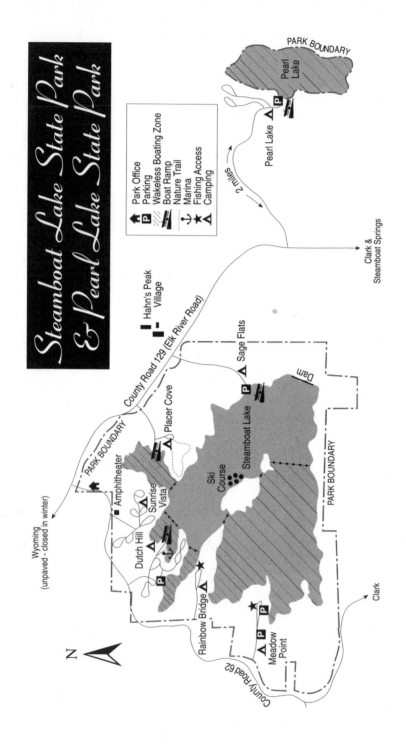

tents and campers or trailers. There are some pullthrough sites in each campground. Only one camping unit per site is allowed.

Campground users must have both a camping permit and a parks pass. Display the camping permit in the plastic holders at the campsites.

Activities: Picnicking is popular at the park. Both Steamboat and Pearl Lake offer excellent fishing opportunities. The coves of Steamboat Lake are well-known for their large rainbow trout. Cutthroat trout dwell in Pearl Lake. Steamboat Lake is the setting for water sports of all kinds. Boaters at both lakes are subject to current Colorado boating statutes and regulations. The use of firearms is prohibited in the summer, but hunting is allowed during the legal seasons. Ice fishing, snowmobiling, cross-country skiing and photography are among the park's most popular winter activities.

Nature: Many kinds of waterfowl nest in the park and in the surrounding marshes. Elk, deer, bear, coyote, fox, beaver, chipmunks, and other small mammals are found in the area. A half-mile nature trail is located at Placer Cove and an amphitheater located at Sunrise Vista is used for interpretive programs during the summer season.

For further information contact: Park Superintendent, Steamboat Lake State Park/Pearl Lake State Park, Box 750, Clark, CO 80428. ☎ (303) 879-3922.

Sweitzer Lake State Park

Location: Three miles W of Delta off US 50 on east Road.

With land donated in 1953 by the Morgan Sweitzer family to what is now the Division of Wildlife, man-made Sweitzer Lake was built for the sole purpose of recreation. Since 1972, the area, with its 137-acre lake and 73 land acres, has been administered by the Colorado Division of Parks and Outdoor Recreation.

Called the "oasis on the edge of the desert," Sweitzer has become a bird-sighting area and a waterfowl observation site for the Audubon Society. About 179 species of birds have been spotted in the area.

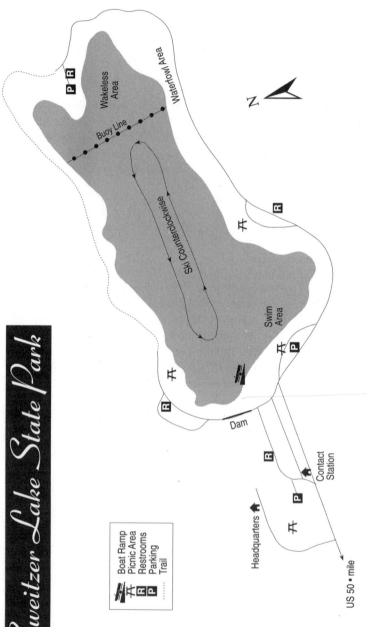

Sweitzer Lake State Park

Wakeless Area

Waterfowl Area

P R

Buoy Line

Ski Counterclockwise

Swim Area

Dam

R

R

R

P

P

Contact Station

Headquarters

US 50 • mile

N

Legend
- Boat Ramp
- Picnic Area
- R Restrooms
- P Parking
- ····· Trail

In the distance, the majestic San Juan Mountains, the Uncompahgre Plateau, and Grand Mesa – the largest flat-top mountain in the world – border Sweitzer Lake. The western edge of the West Elk Mountain Range near Crawford can be seen from the picnic area on the west side of the lake where the environment has been altered with shade trees and grass.

A day-use area with no overnight camping, Sweitzer offers picnicking, swimming, sightseeing, boating, and fishing. The park is open from 8 AM to 5 PM between October 1 and May 1, and from 8 AM to 10 PM from May 1 to September 30.

Boating: Power boating, sailing, and canoeing are popular. A boat ramp is located at the west end of the lake near the dam. Boaters at Sweitzer Lake State Park are subject to Colorado Boating Statutes and Regulations. Brochures are available at the entrance station and park headquarters.

Wildlife/Hunting: A wide variety of small mammals live around Sweitzer. Visitors can view mule deer, rabbits, raccoons, mink, muskrat, and pheasant. The lake provides a haven for many native ducks migratory waterfowl, pelicans, swans, eagles, and much more.

Hunting within the park's boundaries is controlled. Information on seasons and regulations is available from the park headquarters, ☎ (970) 874-4258).

Fishing: Sweitzer Lake, generally considered a good fishing spot for youngsters, contains channel catfish, blue catfish, bluegill, perch, and carp. CAUTION: FISH IN THIS LAKE CONTAIN SELENIUM AND ARE NOT EDIBLE.

Water Sports: Waterskiing, swimming, and scuba diving are popular. Swimming is permitted in the swim area only. Lifeguards are not on duty at the swim area.

Picnicking: Sweitzer is very popular for picnicking because of the many lake-view sites.

Winter Recreation: Cross-county skiing and ice skating are popular winter activities. For more information contact: Park Superintendent, Sweitzer Lake State Park, 1735 E. Road, Delta, CO 81416. ☎ (970) 874-4258.

Sylvan Lake State Park

Location: 16 miles south of Eagle on West Brush Creek Rd.

Sylvan Lake State Park is one of the most beautiful getaways in the state. Nestled in the heart of the majestic Rocky Mountains, it is surrounded by the White River National Forest. The visitor enjoys spectacular 360° panoramic views of the alpine scenery from this 8,500-ft.-high park.

Sylvan Lake is a haven for campers, boaters, picnickers, photographers, and hikers, as well as a base camp for hunters during Colorado's big game hunting season.

The 155-acre park, originally a mink farm, was acquired by the state in 1962 and became part of the Colorado Division of Parks and Outdoor Recreation system in 1987.

Camping: Sylvan Lake State Park has 50 campsites – 30 at Elk Run campground and 20 at Fishermen's Paradise campground. The sites can accommodate tents, trailers and campers, and there are some pull-through sites for larger units. Campers must have a camping permit.

Water Recreation: Only non-motorized boats and electric motors are allowed on the lake.

Fishing: Sylvan Lake is stocked with brook and rainbow trout by the Colorado Division of Wildlife. Fishing is not allowed in the lake inlet and a half mile upstream from September 1 to November 30. It has some of the best year-round trout fishing anywhere.

Hunting: Big game hunting is excellent in the White River National Forest located near the park. Hunting within the park boundaries is controlled. Information on seasons and regulations is available from any park ranger or the park office.

Winter Recreation: Winter enthusiasts come to Sylvan Lake for ice fishing, cross-country skiing, and snowmobiling.

Wildlife: Wildlife watchers can spot mule deer, rabbits, chipmunks, beavers, elk, hummingbirds, and waterfowl throughout the park.

Sylvan Lake State Park

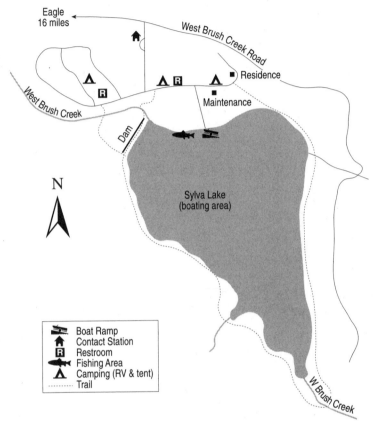

Eagle
16 miles

West Brush Creek Road

West Brush Creek

Dam

Residence

Maintenance

Sylva Lake
(boating area)

N

W Brush Creek

- Boat Ramp
- Contact Station
- Restroom
- Fishing Area
- Camping (RV & tent)
- Trail

For further information contact: Park Superintendent, Sylvan Lake State Park, c/o Rifle Gap State Park, 0050 Road 219, Rifle, CO 81650. ☎ (303) 625-1607.

Trinidad State Park

Location: Three miles west of Trinidad on Colorado 12.

Archaeological finds in and around the park, like the tepee rings in the Carpios Ridge Picnic Area and the mountain branch of the historic Santa Fe Trail, which is now one of Trinidad's main streets, are reminders of the early history of Trinidad State Park.

The dam that created Trinidad Lake was built as an irrigation and flood control project by the US Army Corps of Engineers. The 2,300-acre park, including the 900-acre lake, have been managed by the Colorado Division of Parks and Outdoor Recreation since 1980.

Camping: The 62-site campground can accommodate recreational vehicles, trailers, or tents. Modern facilities include centrally located water hydrants, a coin-operated laundry, electrical hookups, showers, and flush toilets.

Campsites may be reserved in advance at ☎ (800) 678-CAMP.

Please camp only in designated sites and display your camping permit in the site marker. Check-out time is noon. The campground is patrolled for your safety. Quiet after 10 PM.

Picnicking: Picnicking is permitted throughout the park. Group picnic facilities are also available on a reservation basis. Call the park office at ☎ (719) 846-6951 for information.

Boating/Waterskiing: Boaters must observe the Colorado boating statkites and regulations, which are available at the park office and entrances. All boats must observe wakeless speeds around the boat launch area, within 150 ft. of shore fishermen and as buoyed. Boats are not allowed within 200 ft. of the dam or the intake structure, behind the log boom at the lake's west end, and as buoyed.

The water level at Trinidad Lake can fluctuate. Boaters are warned to be especially alert to submerged hazards.

Swimming: Swimming is prohibited at Trinidad State Park.

Fishing: Fishing is permitted anywhere on the lake except the boat launching and docking area. Species caught at Trinidad include rainbow and brown trout, largemouth bass, channel catfish, walleye, crappie, bluegill, and wipers.

Wildlife: Mule deer, coyote, wild turkeys, rabbits, and ground squirrels are frequently seen in the park, along with many other species of birds, reptiles, and small mammals.

Trinidad Lake State Park

N

Trinidad 3 miles

Highway 12

Corps of Engineers Office

South Side Entrance

Ski Counterclockwise

PARK BOUNDARY

PARK BOUNDARY

Wildlife Area

Wildlife Area

NO BOATS

Reilly Canyon Entrance

Cokedale

Highway 12

Boat Ramp
Park Office
Picnic Area
Camping (RV/tent)
Fishing Access
Trail
Wakeless Zone

Hunting: Prohibited in the park between Memorial Day and Labor Day. At other times, hunting is permitted in posted areas during legal seasons. Shotguns or bow and arrows are the only weapons permitted. Information on seasons and regulations is available from a park ranger or the park office.

Hiking/Nature Trails: Two short trails lead from a trailhead located in the campground/picnic area. Neither has water or restroom facilities. The half-mile Carpois Ridge Trail, although steep, offers views of the reservoir and Fishers Peak. The Levsa Canyon Trail contains a one-mile self-guided walk that loops back to the campground area and is perfect for a short informative hike. For the hiking enthusiast, the trail continues four miles farther west to Reality Canyon entrance and the historic town of Cokedale. Across the lake, the two-and-a-half-mile South Shore Trail takes hikers to Long's Canyon and seldom explored areas of the park.

Facilities for Persons with Disabilities: The Carpos Ridge Campground and the picnic area have reserved parking spaces and campsites adapted for persons with disabilities. Restrooms, showers, picnic tables, and drinking fountains are also accessible.

For further information contact: Park Superintendent, Trinidad Lake State Park, 32610 Hwy. 12, Trinidad, CO 81082. ☎ (719) 846-6951.

Vega State Park

Location: NW of Collbran. Exit 1-70 S onto Colorado 65, and then E on Colorado 330 for 12 miles to the park.

*H*igh above the little mountain-town of Collbran lies Vega State Park – 1,830 acres of scenic mountain splendor nestled in the Grand Mesa.

Vega Reservoir and the meadows that surround it are rich in history and natural beauty. The area was originally a mountain meadow where cattle ranchers grazed their herds from the late 1800s until 1962. "Vega" is actually the Spanish word for "meadow."

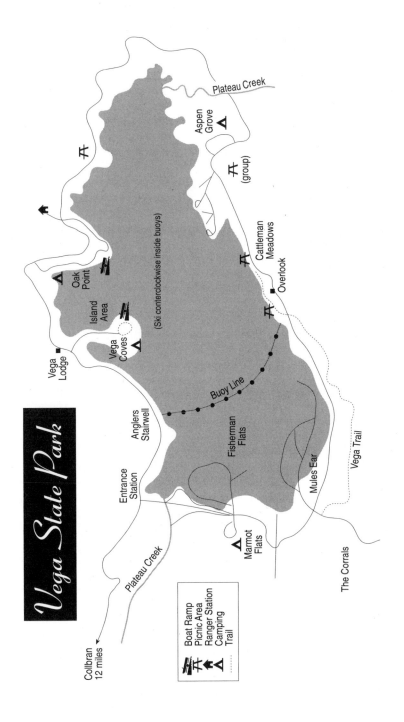

Vega State Park

Plateau Creek

Aspen Grove

⛺ (group)

Cattleman Meadows

⛺ Overlook

(Ski conterclockwise inside buoys)

Oak Point

Island Area

Vega Coves

Buoy Line

Vega Lodge

Anglers Stairwell

Fisherman Flats

Mules Ear

Vega Trail

Entrance Station

Plateau Creek

Marmot Flats

The Corrals

Collbran 12 miles

Boat Ramp
Picnic Area
Ranger Station
Camping
Trail

In 1962, the US Bureau of Reclamation flooded the meadow to build the 900-acre Vega Reservoir. At an elevation of 8,000 ft., this pristine mountain setting quickly became a favorite sport and vacation destination. Snowmobiling and ice fishing have made Vega a well-known winter sports area. Warm-weather visitors include anglers, campers, boaters, waterskiers, and other outdoor enthusiasts.

Visitors throughout the year enjoy Vega's unexpected sub-alpine beauty. Colorado wildflowers and wildlife abound within the park. Visitors are encouraged to enjoy Vega's access to the Grand Mesa park trails; these trails are open to hikers, 4-wheelers, trail bikers, and snowmobilers. There are historical sites to see, including the area where the Dominguez-Escalante expedition camped in 1776, and the Vega cemetery. There is also a ball field here.

Camping: Vega State Park offers 110 individual and group campsites. These can accommodate RV's, tents, and campers. Sites are available on a first-come, first-served basis, or you can reserve a special site by calling, in Denver, ☎ (303) 470-1144 or, outside Denver, ☎ (800) 678-CAMP.

Boats/Water Sports: Waterskiing season at the park usually begins in early June and ends by mid-August, depending on the water level. Windsurfers and jet skiers are welcome. The waters are refreshing during the Grand Valley's 100° temperatures in August.

Picnicking: The park has many individual sites and one group picnic shelter which accommodates 100-200 people.

Fishing: Vega Reservoir is about two miles long when full. It is the largest body of water in the Grand Valley region. Because Vega is about 2,000 ft. lower in elevation than Grand Mesa, it is the last to freeze in the fall and the first to thaw in the spring. Few lakes anywhere can surpass the Vega Reservoir as a trout fishery.

Wildlife: Deer, elk, beaver, and many kinds of waterfowl frequent Vega. Also found here are weasel, rabbits, chipmunks, hawks, blue grouse, and the elusive wild turkey. Coyotes and bobcats are known in the area.

Nature Trail: A self-guiding nature trail with interpretive view stations leads walkers through aspen forests and other high altitude vegetation.

Motorized Recreation: A trail for 4-wheelers and dirt bikes leads from Vega State Park to Grand Mesa and is especially popular in the fall.

Winter Recreation: Cold weather enthusiasts come to Vega State Park for ice fishing, ice skating, snowmobiling, cross-country skiing, and snow play.

For further information contact: Park Superintendent, Vega State Parks, Box 186, Collbran, CO 81624, ☎ (303) 487-3407.

National Parks

Mesa Verde National Park

Location: High plateau country of southwestern Colorado. The park entrance is between Cortez and Mancos, off US 160. It is 21 miles from the entrance to park headquarters and the Chaplin Mesa ruins. Morefield campground is four miles from the entrance; Far View Visitor Center is 15 miles. Allow at least 45 minutes for the drive to Chapin Mesa.

About 1,400 years ago, long before any European exploration of the New World, a group of Indians living in the Four Corners region chose Mesa Verde for their home. For over 700 years their descendants lived and flourished here, eventually building elaborate stone cities in the sheltered recesses of the canyon walls. Then in the late 1200s, within the span of one or two generations, they abandoned their homes.

Mesa Verde National Park, which occupies part of a large plateau rising high above the Montezuma and Mancos Valleys, preserves a spectacular remnant of their 1,000-year-old culture. These people are known as the Anasazi, from a Navajo word meaning "the ancient ones." Ever since local cowboys discovered the cliff dwellings a century ago, archaeologists have been trying to understand the life of these people. But despite decades of excavation, analysis, classification, and comparison, knowledge is still sketchy. No one knows the whole story of their existence, for they left no written records and much that was important in their lives has perished. Certain information may still be gleaned from the ruins. These people were adept at building, artistic in the crafts, and skillful at wrestling a living from a difficult land. They accumulated skills and traditions and passed them on from one generation to another over the centuries. By classic times (AD 1100-1300), the Anasazi of Mesa Verde were the heirs of a vigorous civilization, with accomplishments in communal living and arts that rank among the finest expressions of human culture in ancient America.

Taking advantage of nature, the Anasazi built their dwellings below the overhanging cliffs. Their basic construction material was sandstone, which they shaped into rectangular blocks about the size of a loaf of bread. The mortar between the blocks was a mix of mud and water. Rooms averaged about 6" x 8" – space enough for two or three persons. Isolated rooms in the rear and on the upper levels were generally used for storing crops.

Much of the daily routine took place in the open courtyards in front of the rooms. The women fashioned pottery, while the men made various tools – knives, axes, awls, scrapers – out of stone and bone. The fires built in summer were mainly for cooking. In winter when the alcove rooms were damp and uncomfortable, fires probably burned throughout the village. Smoke-blackened walls and ceilings are reminders of the biting cold these people lived with for half of every year.

Clothing followed the seasons. In summer, the people wore simple loincloths and sandals. In winter, they dressed in hides and skins and wrapped themselves against the cold in blankets made of turkey feathers and robes of rabbit fur.

Getting food was a ceaseless struggle, even in the best of years. Farming was the main business of these people, but they supplemented their crops of corn, beans, and squash by gathering wild plants and hunting deer, rabbits, squirrels, and other game. Their only domestic animals were dogs and turkeys.

Fortunately for us, the Anasazi tossed their trash close by. Scraps of food, broken pottery and tools, anything unwanted went down the slope in front of their houses. Much of what we know about their daily life here comes from these garbage heaps.

The Anasazi Family

The structure of Anasazi life is difficult to know. Archaeology has yielded some information, but without written documents, there is no way to be sure about their social, political, or religious ideas. Comparisons with the modern Pueblo people of New Mexico and Arizona are revealing. In classic times at Mesa Verde, several generations probably lived together as a household. Each family occupied several rooms and built additional ones as it grew. Several related families constituted a clan, which may have been matrilineal (descent through the female line) in organization. Each clan may have had its own kiva, or ceremonial room, and rights to its own agricultural plots.

History

The first Anasazi settled in Mesa Verde (Spanish for "green table") about AD 550. They are known as Basketmakers because of their impressive skill at that craft. Formerly a nomadic people, they were beginning to lead a more settled way of life. Farming replaced hunting and gathering as their main source of livelihood. They lived in pithouses clustered into small villages, which they usually built on the mesa tops but occasionally in the cliff recesses. They learned how to make pottery and they acquired the bow and arrow, a more efficient weapon for hunting than the atlatl or spear thrower.

These were fairly prosperous times for the Basketmakers, and their population multiplied. About 750 AD they began building houses above ground, with upright walls made of poles and mud. They built these houses one against another in long, curving rows, often with a pithouse or two in front. The pithouses were probably the forerunners of the kivas of later times. From this time on, these people are known as *Pueblos*, a Spanish word for village dwellers.

By 1000 AD the Anasazi had advanced from pole-and-adobe construction to skillful stone masonry. Their walls of thick, double-coursed stone often rose two or three stories high and were joined together into units of 50 rooms or more. Pottery also changed, as black drawings on a white background replaced crude designs on dull gray. Farming provided more of the diet than before, and much mesa-top land was cleared for that purpose.

The years from 1100-1300 AD were Mesa Verde's classic period. The population may have reached several thousand. It was mostly concentrated in compact villages of many rooms, often with the kivas built inside the enclosing walls rather than out in the open. Round towers began to appear, and there was a rising level of craftsmanship in masonry work, pottery, weaving, jewelry and even tool-making. The stone walls of the large pueblos are regarded as the finest ever built in Mesa Verde; they are made of carefully shaped stones laid up in straight courses. Baskets show evidence of a decline in workmanship, but this may be due to the widespread use of pottery and consequent decrease in attention to the craft. About 1200 AD there was another major population shift. The Anasazi began to move back into the cliff alcoves that had sheltered their ancestors long centuries before. The reason for this is unknown. Perhaps it was for defense; perhaps the caves offered better protection from the elements; perhaps there were religious or psychological reasons. Whatever the reason, it gave rise to the cliff dwellings for which Mesa Verde is famous.

Most of the cliff dwellings were built in the middle decades of the 1200s. They range in size from one-room houses to villages of over 200 rooms (Cliff Palace). Architecturally, there is no standard ground plan. The builders fitted their structures to the available space. Most walls were single courses of stone, perhaps because the alcove roofs limited heights and also protected them from erosion by the weather. The masonry work varied in quality – rough construction can be found alongside walls with well-shaped stones. Many rooms were plastered on the inside and decorated with painted designs. The Anasazi lived in the cliff houses for less than 100 years.

Flourishing settlements must have dotted Wetherill Mesa. Thousands of acres of flat mesa top land were available for the cultivation of corn, beans, and squash, the staple crops throughout Mesa Verde. A yearly average of 18 inches of moisture enhanced the deep, rich soil and nourished the varied vegetation during drought years water storage reservoirs and check dams ensured at least a minimal harvest. Nearly 1,000 of these check dams were constructed. In fact, near Step House a series of 100 terraces within only a quarter mile have been found.

We know that the last quarter of the century was a time of drought and crop failures. In the fragile pinyon pine-juniper ecosystem of Mesa Verde, constant occupation and land use eventually took its toll. As the population expanded, pressure from over-farming decreased the productivity of the fields. Extensive clearing and use of trees for both construction and firewood could have depleted the valuable timber resource. The game animals were probably reduced in number due to hunting. These pressures, in combination with the serious drought of the late 1200s, created an environment in which the Anasazi could survive no longer. Gradually, families abandoned their homes and moved elsewhere.

When the Anasazi left, they may have traveled south into New Mexico and Arizona, perhaps settling among their kin already there. Whatever happened, it seems likely that some Pueblo Indians today are descendants of the cliff dwellers of the Mesa Verde.

Visiting the Park

To get the most out of your visit, go first to either the Far View Visitor Center (open only in the summer) or to the Chapin Mesa Museum (open from 8 AM to 6:30 PM in summer and 8 AM to 5 PM the rest of the year). Rangers there will help you plan your visit.

Morefield campground, open early spring through late fall, has single and group campsites. Campsites for the physically impaired are available. All campsites have a table, benches, and grill. Gathering firewood or injuring trees and shrubs is prohibited. Camps should not be left unattended for more than 24 hours. Some utility hookups are available, and there is a dump station for RVs. Near the park entrance are several commercial campgrounds.

Services at the campground include groceries, carry-out food, gasoline, firewood, showers, and a laundromat. Evening campfire programs are given daily from early June to September. During the summer non-denominational religious services are held. Three hiking trails originate in the Morefield area.

Park Point offers superb views of the entire Four Corners region. The fire lookout station here is staffed during the fire season. A brochure describes the natural features of the area.

Far View is a major center of visitor service. The visitor center, open from late spring through mid-autumn, displays contemporary Indian arts and crafts. Commercial tours of Chapin Mesa leave from Far View Motor Lodge. The motor lodge is open from May through October. For reservations, write ARA Mesa Verde Company, Box

277, Mancos, Colorado 81328. ☎ 529-4421. There is a restaurant at the lodge and a cafeteria nearby. Gasoline is available.

Wetherill Mesa is accessible during the summer by private vehicle between the hours of 8 AM and 4:30 PM. Vehicles over 8,000 pounds GVW and/or over 25 ft. in length are prohibited. The 12-mile mountain road to Wetherill has sharp curves and steep grades.

Please obey the posted speed limits. Roadside pullouts offer spectacular views of the Four Corners region. Two cliff dwellings, Step House and Long House, are open to the public. Badger House Community, a mesa-top complex near Long House, is accessible over, three-quarter-mile trail. Rangers are on duty to interpret the sites. You can buy sandwiches and cold drinks at Wetherill.

Wetherill Mesa, forming part of the western boundary of Mesa Verde National Park, contains the second largest concentration of ruins in the area.

Chapin Mesa: Three major cliff dwellings on Chapin Mesa – Spruce Tree House, Cliff Palace, and Balcony House – are open in season for visits, and many others are visible from Ruins Road. An archaeological museum with dioramas interprets the life of the ancient Anasazi. In summer, rangers conduct tours through some of the cliff dwellings. Current schedules are available at the museum or Far View Visitor Center.

Two hiking trails lead into Spruce Canyon. The Petroglyph Point Trail, 2.8 miles, and Spruce Canyon Trail, 2.1 miles, begin at points on the Spruce Tree House Trail. Hikers must register at the ranger's office before attempting these trails.

Other cliff dwellings can be seen from canyon-rim vantage points by taking the self-guiding loop drives of Ruins Road. Wayside exhibits interpret the development of Anasazi culture from Basketmakers through the Classic period. These roads are open from 8 AM until sunset. During winter, the mesa-top loops are open as weather permits. Visitors may snowshoe or cross-country ski on roadways. Check at the museum for information and conditions. Cliff dwellings are closed and cannot be entered.

In winter, rangers lead guided tours (three a day) of Spruce Tree House, weather and trail conditions permitting. Spruce Tree Terrace, selling light snacks, gifts, and souvenirs, is open year-round.

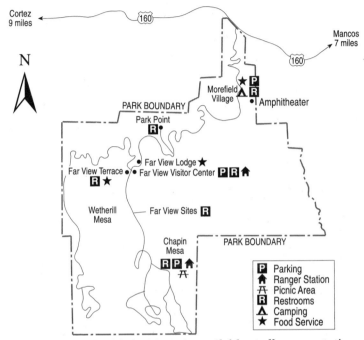

A guidebook for disabled visitors is available at all ranger stations, the visitor center, and the museum.

Note: Visits to cliff dwellings are strenuous. Altitudes in the park may vary from 6,000 to 8,500 ft. Trails may be uneven; steps and ladders must frequently be climbed. Hiking or touring cliff dwellings is not recommended for persons with heart or respiratory ailments. You can view most of the major cliff dwellings from overlooks.

Balcony House

Balcony House may be the highlight of a visit to Mesa Verde National Park. There is no other site open to the public where people have so much fun climbing ladders, crawling through a tunnel, and generally exploring an entire cliff dwelling. Tucked under a sandstone overhang 600 feet above the floor of Soda Canyon, Balcony House faces east. A medium-sized cliff dwelling containing 35-40 rooms, it housed 40-50 people. It was built by the Anasazi in the early 1200s. Like other cliff dwellings in Mesa Verde, it was occupied for 75-100 years. Visitors marvel at its fine stone-work, original plaster, balcony, and wooden timbers, and its defen-sive location. Similar building techniques are still found in the villages of the Pueblo Indians in New Mexico and Arizona. Anthro-pologists believe that these modern people are the descendants of the Anasazi. Much of the information we use to interpret Anasazi customs is based on these Pueblo people's traditions because so many of their practices continue into the twentieth century.

A prospector named S.E. Osborn is generally given credit for dis-covering Balcony House. In 1884, he came up Soda Canyon looking for coal deposits. There is no record of whether he found the coal, but he did discover the dwelling. Originally called "Brownstone Front," it was not until 1891 that Gustaf Nordenskiold, a Swedish explorer who wrote one of the first books about Mesa Verde, gave the dwelling its present name. When you enter the first (north) courtyard of the dwelling, you can clearly see why Balcony House is such an appropriate name. The balcony there is in excellent shape. It was used to enter the second story rooms. People might work on the balcony, watch their children, or simply look off across the canyon. Not many original balconies remain in such good condition, but they seem to have been common, especially in the larger sites.

Cliff Palace

Cliff Palace is the largest cliff dwelling in North America. In 1906 the United States Congress established Mesa Verde National Park to preserve the extensive archaeological resources in the region. Please treat these sites with care to preserve them for future visi-tors. Numbered markers along the trail will show you where to make the various stops.

Take a minute to note the overall features of Cliff Palace. The upper ledge contains remnants of 14 storage rooms ranging between 39-42 inches in height (1 to 1.2 meters). The Anasazi gained access to these storage rooms by using a short ladder to the small doorway on the far left. You can see two notches below the doorway where the top of the ladder rested. Such storage rooms may seem incon-veniently placed, yet they were quite practical because they were cool, dry, and out of the way of children and domesticated dogs and turkeys. Since this wall section was made using only carefully stacked rocks without mortar, it is known as "dry wall." Perhaps the Anasazi built it during a time when water scarcity prevented the use of mortar, or it may have been built as an emergency repair procedure. In 1934 the National Park Service stabilized the area around the large boulder which contains several vertical cracks. This section has been reinforced with over 70 tons (6,360 kilos) of steel and concrete, hidden by the wall beneath the boulder. Prehistoric masonry was found beneath the boulder during stabilization. Obviously, the Anasazi were also concerned with keeping this rock in place.

Doorways in the cliff dwellings were probably built deliberately small to keep out the cold air and drafts of the winter months. At such times, the Anasazi covered them with rectangular sandstone slabs about an inch thick. During the summer months, they placed willow mats, skins or hides over the doorways for privacy. Often people look at the size of these doorways and wonder about the size of the Anasazi. An average man was about 5'4" to 5'5" tall, while an average woman was 5' to 5'1". If you compared them with the European people of the same time period, they would have been about the same size.

The main construction material was sandstone. The Anasazi chipped and pecked the sandstone with harder, riverbed stones. The mortar between the blocks is a mud and water mixture. Over the top, the Anasazi placed a thin coating of plaster, which was the first to erode as time passed.

Residents of Cliff Palace carried water to the dwelling from several nearby springs. The closest spring today is across the canyon below Sun Temple.

Spruce Tree House

This is an area that has changed very little in 700-800 years. To the Anasazi, the canyons provided food, shelter and other materials for daily survival. Some of the most important plants to the people of Spruce Tree House are located just down the trail.

Spruce Tree House, the third largest cliff dwelling among several hundred within park boundaries (Cliff Palace and Long House are larger), was constructed between AD 1200 and 1276 by the Anasazi. The dwelling contains about 114 rooms and eight kivas built into a natural cave measuring 216 ft. (66 meters) at its greatest depth. It is thought to have been home for about 100 people.

Spruce Tree House was opened for visitation following excavation by Dr. Jesse Walter Fewkes of the Smithsonian Institution. Dr. Fewkes removed the debris of fallen walls and roofs and stabilized the walls approximately as you see them now. Due to the protection of the overhanging cliff, Spruce Tree House had deteriorated very little through the years and has required little supportive maintenance.

The cliff dwelling was first reported in 1888, when two local ranchers chanced upon it while searching for stray cattle. A large tree, which they identified as a Douglas spruce, was found growing from the front of the dwelling to the mesa top. It is said that the men first entered the ruin by climbing down this tree, which was later cut down by another early explorer.

Park Point

Park Point, the highest elevation on the Mesa, offers an unobstructed 360° panoramic view of the area. Depending on atmospheric conditions, which vary with the amount of man-made contamination, natural haze and time of year, the view in any direction is truly breathtaking. The park Point area is a favorite spot for park visitors who enjoy drawing, sketching, painting, and photography.

Park Point is surrounded on the north by Mount Wilson and Lone Cone, on the east by the La Plata Range, on the south by the Hogback, Shiprock and Lukachukai Mountains, and on the west by the Montezuma Valley and Sleeping Ute Mountain. In the distance to the northwest one can view the Abajo and Manti-La Sal mountains in Utah. The San Juan mountains and the rugged canyon and mesa country form an outstanding backdrop for the large concentration of prehistoric Pueblo ruins located within the park. These scenic views contribute to the total experience of Mesa Verde and the remnants of the culture that lived here.

Fire Lookout

This tower is manned by a National Park Service Ranger during the critical fire season.

The ranger watches for fires, which are most likely after thunderstorms. The ranger is on the lookout for telltale columns of smoke. When smoke is spotted, a sighting, or azimuth, is taken with an instrument called an Osborne Firefinder. The ranger lines up the smoke-site through the sight of the firefinder and reads the compass degree of the fire.

To confirm the reading requested assistance is received from another tower in the park. This ranger also spots the fire and gets a degree reading from the firefinder. The readings are then called into the dispatcher in the park ranger's office and a triangulation is made from which the fire can be located on the map. A report is then called in by description: color, estimated size, wind direction, and possible fuels that are burning. The park will then estimate the size of the fire and manpower required for suppression.

The ranger also has the responsibility of projecting weather conditions and the possibility of fire resulting from these conditions.

The National Park Service cooperates with the Bureau of Indian Affairs and the Bureau of Land Management to protect the park and surrounding lands from potential wildfires.

The Mesa

The mesa for which Mesa Verde National Park is named is an erosional remnant rising above the surrounding Dolores Plateau. This high tableland is intricately dissected by steep-walled canyons. From Park Point the surface slopes downward to the south into a bowl-shaped amphitheater from an elevation of about 8,600 ft. to 6,000 ft. at the southern end of the park. No active water sources other than springs are present in the park.

A three-mile round-trip loop trail introduces the Indian petroglyphs and natural environment at Mesa Verde National Park. Allow two or three hours for the trip.

Mesa Verde National Park has a wealth of natural history in the variety of its plant and animal life and its interesting geology. All of these elements are interwoven with the prehistoric Indian civilization which centered on the mesa from around AD 600 to AD 1300. The Indian people had a tremendous understanding of their natural environment and the use of that environment to fulfill needs of food, shelter, and clothing.

In the centuries that elapsed between the abandonment of Mesa Verde and entrance of white men into the Southwest, there was little change in the material culture of the Pueblo Indians. These people, who live in northern Arizona and New Mexico, are probably the descendants of the Anasazi who lived here in Mesa Verde. It is from records of the early explorers and missionaries and later from reports of early ethnologists who studied the Pueblos that we derive the reconstruction of Mesa Verde life.

On this trail you will be introduced to the natural environment of Mesa Verde and ways in which it was used by the Indians. This loop trail is about three miles (4.8 km) in length and returns you to the headquarters area.

Establishment of Mesa Verde National Park

Mesa Verde National Park's establishment has a unique and colorful history. It was created largely through the efforts of a private group of women. As one early article stated, "It is noteworthy that to a woman's patient, unremitting work and unfaltering loyalty to an idea, the nation owes this new study ground and playground for its citizens." Two women figure most prominently in the attempt to preserve the cliff dwellings – Virginia McClurg and Lucy Peabody. They must share the honor of being the "Mother of Mesa Verde." They conducted an extensive speaking and writing campaign to awaken the public to the necessity of preserving these sites. In 1900, the Colorado Cliff Dwelling Association was created. Its object was the restoration and preservation of the ruins and the dissemination of knowledge concerning these prehistoric people. The women continued their lobbying in Congress until 1906. At last Theodore Roosevelt signed the bill establishing Mesa Verde National Park.

Caphin Mesa Archaeological Museum

The Archaeological Museum on Chapin Mesa contains superb examples of prehistoric artifacts of the American Southwest.

Its beginnings, however, were modest, for it started as one of the rooms in a two-room log cabin. It was initially intended to be a ranger station, but the increasing need for a display area for artifacts became a priority. In 1917, Superintendent Thomas Rickner set aside $22 for a display case, and by 1918 the log cabin museum was opened to the public.

The success of the log cabin museum clearly demonstrated the need for a larger facility at Mesa Verde. When Superintendent Jesse L. Nusbaum began his administration of the park in 1921, he immediately began a campaign to have a large museum built to replace the original log cabin museum.

Through the interest and generosity of Mrs. Stella Leviston and, later, John D. Rockefeller, Jr., sufficient funds were acquired for the museum, which was completed in 1925. More work brought the museum to its present form by 1936.

The exhibits at the Archaeological Museum on Chapin Mesa begin with a set of dioramas that depict the development of the Indians of the Mesa Verde. The archaeological authenticity of the miniatures (as well as the sensitivity and humorous vignettes displayed) can be credited, in part, to their creators, Alfred Lee Rowell and Don Watson.

Rowell came to Mesa Verde in 1936 to begin work on the dioramas and refurbish existing ones. Rowell and Civilian Conservation Corps workers completed the displays in 1940.

The dioramas provide an overview of the culture of Mesa Verde that cannot be conveyed in words, nor even by visiting the sites themselves.

The exhibits and displays at the museum enhance the understanding of the sites found in the park, and will deepen your appreciation of the development of the ancient culture of the Mesa Verde. You may want to make this your first stop.

At the museum information desk, a ranger is available to answer questions. A wheelchair and portable ramp are available upon request to aid accessibility to the exhibits. Within the museum the Mesa Verde Museum Association operates a bookstore, which has more than 400 titles on ancient Puebloan and Southwestern topics.

The National Register of Historic Places

Mesa Verde National Park was placed on the National Register of Historic Places in 1966 in recognition of the significance of its development as part of the National Park System.

The sensitivity, dedication, and knowledge of the early park administrators were essential to the development of Mesa Verde. The early buildings in the park Headquarters area are still in use. These buildings were constructed between 1920 and 1930 under the direction of Jesse Nusbaum, the park superintendent. All are built in a generalized Pueblo Indian style called "Mesa Verde Modified Pueblo." The same type of local sandstone used in these modern buildings was used in the prehistoric structures. This, combined with the construction technique, creates a sense of balance between the landscape and the buildings.

At the time he conceived the design of the buildings, Nusbaum wrote: "In taking the liberty of suggesting this type of construction it seems the most logical for many reasons. The material necessary for the construction is right on the ground and easily accessible. This type will not detract one iota from the ancient dwellings but will help to preserve the Indian atmosphere which the ruins and environment create."

Lodging

The Far View Lodge is open April 21-October 20. Walk-ins are welcome.

If simple pleasures appeal to you, consider spending a night or two at the lodge. No phones, no TVs – just great dining, evening programs, and star gazing off your private balcony.

Camping

Morefield Campground is open April 29-October 16. Campsites are always available. With more than 400 sites, Morefield has been completely filled only once in 10 years. Campsites loop through a tranquil, green valley that is as much home to deer and wild turkeys as to human visitors. Some areas are set aside for recreational vehicles and tent campers. Services at the campground include coin-operated hot showers, laundry,a well-stocked grocery and campers' store.

For further information contact: Park Superintendent, Mesa Verde National Park, CO 81330. ☎ (303) 529-4465.

Rocky Mountain National Park

Location: North of the mining towns of Colorado's central Rockies, and just northwest of the city of Boulder.

Rocky Mountain National Park preserves the beauty of the flora and fauna of the Rockies, as they were before settlers began pouring into Colorado from the east during the 1800s.

The 410 square miles of park contain abundant wildlife, 700 species of wildflowers, and 150 secluded alpine lakes. There is also a 13-mile stretch above the timberline that contain sites similar to those found above the Arctic Circle.

Rocky Mountain National Park allows people of all abilities the opportunity to experience wilderness and wildlife. In recent years, special efforts by park partners and park staff have provided for the greater enjoyment of the visiting public while preserving the natural conditions and scenic beauties of the national park. For example, the Sprague Lake Nature Trail allows a complete stroll around the lake for seniors, visitors with disabilities, and families with small children. Another park improvement includes a boardwalk with trailside exhibits along Hidden Valley Beaver Ponds. A free publication, *Access Rocky,* provides more information on services available in the park.

Trail Ridge Road (US Hwy. 34)
Open late May-October, depending on weather. Connects Grand Lake and Estes Park and climbs to more than 12,000 ft. (3,657 m) above sea level. People with respiratory or heart ailments should consult their physician.

To Estes Park
65 miles (104 km or 1½ hours) northwest of Denver. Take US Hwy 34 or US Hwy 36.

To Grand Lake
85 miles (136 km or 2 hours) west of Denver. Take interstate 70 to Exit #232. To Granby via US Hwy 40, then north 16 miles (26 km) on US Hwy 34 to Grand Lake.

Visitor Centers

Visitor Center/Headquarters (7840')
2½ miles (4 km) west of Estes Park on US Hwy 36. Open daily year-round.

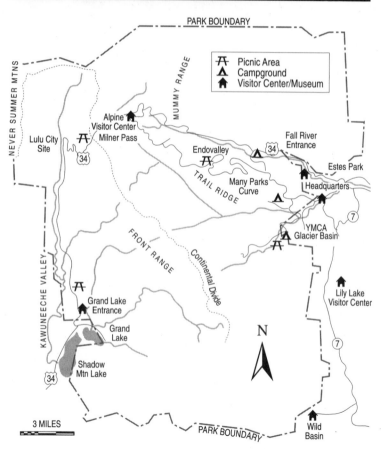

Kawuneeche Visitor Center (8720')
1.3 miles, (2.1 km) north of Grand Lake on US Hwy. 34. Open daily year-round.

Moraine Park Museum (8140')
5 miles (8 km) west of Estes Park on Bear Lake Road. Open daily May through mid-October.

Alpine Visitor Center (11,796')
25 miles (40 km) west of Estes Park on Trail Ridge Road. Open daily June through mid-October.

Lily Lake Visitor Center (8930')
6 miles (9.6 km) south of Estes Park on Colorado Hwy 7. Open daily June through August.

Back Country Camping/Bivouac Camping

Permit always required. Write to the back country Office, c/o Rocky Mountain National Park, Estes Park, CO 80517. ☎ (303) 586-1242

Accomodations/Services

There are no accommodations in the park, besides campgrounds.

For information on motels, lodges, or cabins, call the Estes Park Chamber of Commerce at ☎ (800) 443-7837 or Grand Lake Chamber of Commerce at ☎ (800) 531-1019.

Wildlife: Mule deer, wapiti (American elk), and bighorn sheep are seen frequently. Coyote, black bear, mountain lion, and bobcat are native in the area. Moose, reintroduced to the North Park area in 1978, are commonly seen in the Kawuneeche Valley.

Fishing: A Colorado state fishing license is required. Bear Lake is closed to fishing. Other restrictions exist.

Horseback Riding: Guided rides are conducted by liveries located inside and outside the park. Private stock are welcome and trails are listed in a special publication called *Horses and Other Pack Animals*.

Hiking: Over 355 miles of hiking trails are maintained. Please don't "shortcut" the efforts; stay on the trails to prevent erosion and preserve the vegetation and soil.

Ranger Programs: Schedules of ranger-led walks and talks are listed in the park newspaper.

Private Campgrounds: There are privately operated campgrounds in the towns of Estes Park and Grand Lake. A few offer public showers.

For further information contact: Park Superintendent, Rocky Mountain National Park, Estes Park, CO 80517. ☎ (303) 586-1206 or (303) 586-1333 (recording).